250 Things to Do in Cyprus on a Sunny Day*

by Chris Alden

* ... or a rainy one. They happen, you know.

Published in 2012 by
Islebright Books & eBooks.

ISBN 978-0-9573648-0-6

www.islebright.com

Contents

How to use this book

Welcome. This is a guidebook suggesting the best things to do in Cyprus – island of sun, sea, scenery and no few surprises. It's a book for people who love to get off the beaten track and explore – but who also want insider tips to guide them along the way.

The book is mainly organised by region. The first six chapters of the book correspond to six areas of the island, as numbered on this map:[1]

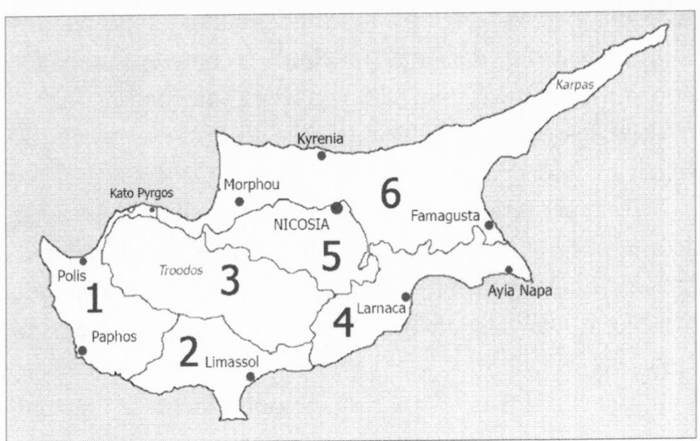

Map adapted from OpenStreetMap © OpenStreetMap contributors, CC BY-SA

1: Paphos, including the resort area of Paphos in the south-west, and the Akamas peninsula on the north-west tip;

2: Limassol, including Limassol city, its hill villages, the ancient ruins at Curium and the Akrotiri peninsula;

3: Troodos, including the high Troodos mountains, and the Paphos Forest and Machairas Forest to the west and east;

4: Larnaca and Ayia Napa, including the city of Larnaca, resort of Ayia Napa, and nature trails at Cape Greco;

5: Nicosia, covering the walled city of Nicosia south of the Green Line – that is, the line of *de facto* partition that has been in place since the Turkish invasion in 1974 – and areas south and west of the city;

6: the north, covering the Turkish Cypriot administered area north of the Green Line. The area includes Morphou, the rest of Nicosia, Kyrenia, Karpas, the walled city of Famagusta, and the ancient ruins at Salamis.

There is also another chapter at the end of the book:

7: Things to do anywhere. If you are looking for themed activities – sporty, arty or in the great outdoors – or just want to know about the food and drink of the island, this is the chapter for you. It also includes recommendations for a good road map to bring with you when you come.

Listings often include web links to external resources, which are intended to be useful.[2]

The book is intended to be used in conjunction with a decent road map – see page 128 for a couple of suggestions.

One final note: this book has been written out of a love for Cyprus – an island which, despite its flaws, just seems to grab people and keep them coming back. So have fun in Cyprus – and if you have any suggestions, do get in touch.

1. Things to do in Paphos

A neat little fort overlooking the picturesque harbour of Katopaphos; some of the most ornate Roman mosaics in the Mediterranean; ancient rock tombs, the supposed birthplace of Aphrodite and good, family-friendly beaches.

With so many picture-postcard sights, is it any wonder that tourists come in their droves to the Paphos region of Cyprus?

But perhaps the most rewarding thing about Paphos is its rural beauty when you get off the beaten track. If you love countryside, then the Akamas peninsula, on the north-west tip of the island, is a natural wonder with isolated beaches and a carpet of wildflowers in spring.

You'll never tire, either, of exploring the hill villages of the Laona region, north of Kathikas; or the wineries and ancient trails near Pano Panayia. And if you like to get away from it all, Kato Pyrgos, on the north coast, is a resort for people who like to take things easier than most.

Paphos old town (Ktima)

The once-sleepy old town of Paphos (official spelling: Pafos[3]), also known as Ktima, is a workaday hub with a traffic problem. But don't neglect it: it has a smart neoclassical centre, and dotted around are some great places to eat, shop and watch the world go by.

Have lunch in a back-street restaurant.

Possibly the most obvious reason to come up to the old town of Paphos is for a decent lunch. And happily, on a back street just off the main Makarios III shopping street (near what used to be the fruit and veg market) is **Laona** (+357 26 937121, www.laonarestaurant.blogspot.co.uk) – a deservedly popular restaurant serving good-quality home cooking for the lunchtime crowd. Because it's on a quiet street, you can happily eat inside or outside.

Eat and drink at Politeia.

Just south-west of the huge, neoclassical town hall in the centre of Paphos (popular for civil weddings) is a street known variously as October 28 Square and Iakovou Iakovides Street. On the little roundabout at the end, Costis Palamas Square, **Politeia** (+357 26 222288) is a chilled-out cafe-bar aimed at younger Cypriots that's good both for food and for a late-night drink.

Wander down past Ayios Theodoros for the view.

Just off the roundabout with the Politeia cafe on it, there's an unassuming little back street called Andrea Ioannou, which heads down toward Ayios Theodoros, Paphos' cathedral. At the bottom of the street, just past the church (which you can stick your head in and explore), you arrive at a little square on a clifftop, with a view down to Katopaphos.

On the square here, there's a cafe called **Muse** (+357 26 941951, www.muse-kitchen-bar.com), which is a good place to take in the vista.

Heading downhill from the square, with the Axiothea hotel on your left, you soon reach the **Paphos Municipal Gallery** (+357 26 930653, www.visitpafos.org.cy/ municipal_gallery.aspx). This small, free museum hosts the work of artists from the town.

Try a neighbourhood souvlaki.

For the uninitiated, *souvlaki* is Greek for kebab – but a souvlaki in Cyprus, thankfully, has little in common with what passes for a late-night snack in the cities of Britain.

There are neighbourhood *souvlaki* shops all over Cyprus, and you can have fun experimenting until you find one you like – but one good option I know is the **unnamed souvlaki place** on Akropoleos Street, just on the left after you turn off Nikolaou Nikolaidi. What you get here is a large, fluffy, toasted Cyprus pitta, liberally filled with cubed pork, tomato, onion, flat leaf parsley, lemon juice and salt. What's great about it is the way the pork juices, citric acid and salt combine with the fluffy interior of the Cyprus pitta – delicious.

As an option, you can also have *souvlaki-sheftalia*, which is 50% pork cubes, 50% Cyprus sausage.

Send a postcard at the old post office.

Of course, no one sends postcards any more – but if you're looking for a reason to buck the trend, the **old post office**, on Nikodimou Mylona Street in central Ktima, provides it. This old building with its Venetian-style shutters is an echo of the country's colonial past.

Visit the Ottoman baths.

Built in the 16th century after the arrival of the Ottoman Turks, the **Ottoman baths** (www.visitpafos.org.cy/ottoman_baths.aspx) were a community centre in the town for centuries. After their closure to the public in the 20th century, they were somewhat forgotten – but they've been restored recently, and are now used as a cultural centre for the municipality. You'll find them in the centre of the old town, on the seaward side of the old market.

Browse for jewellery at SmartRocks.

There are so many Cypriot-run jewellery shops in Paphos that it might seem odd to recommend one owned by a Brit. But **SmartRocks** (+357 26 222346, www.smartrockspaphos.com), which occupies a tiny little shop in a little arcade just off the main shopping street, is distinctive because it's also the jeweller's workshop. Here you'll get one-to-one attention and find some great one-off pieces to buy.

Go browsing for a Cyprus barbecue – known as a foukou.

This is completely impractical, of course – given what airlines charge for hold baggage, the idea of lugging an entire Cypriot barbecue home with you must seem very strange. But if you've ever seen a Cypriot operating a *foukou*, you might just be tempted. The principle is that, after lighting the fire and threading the meat on the skewers, the operator of the *foukou* does virtually nothing: the machine does all the work, with battery-controlled motors rotating the skewers, so browning the meat evenly. Cue Keo and kudos.

In Paphos, you can go *foukou*-shopping in the older quarter of the town – I bought mine from a place called **Zootrofos Kyknos**, run by Nikos Papanikolas at Thermopylae 66 – but there are other shops in the immediate area too. Prices range from under €100 for a souvlaki-only model to perhaps €200 for a fully adjustable one (which allows you to raise and lower even the smallest skewers, in order to control the distance of the meat from the coals) – but goods may be unmarked, and negotiation is often the order of the day.

Cyprus is such a barbecue-obsessed country that you can even find replacement *foukou* motors in the typical *periptero* (corner shop kiosk), so if your motor breaks while you are cooking the Easter *souvla* (chunks of lamb), you can dash to the shop and buy another one. This actually happened to me. Other countries are not so civilised – so if, like me, you send a *foukou* abroad, pack a spare motor.

Visit the Paphos Archaeological Museum.

The Paphos Archaeological Museum (+357 26 306215, www.visitpafos.org.cy/Paphos_Archaeological_Museum.aspx) is an unglamorous building in an unglamorous suburb – but it's a good introduction to the chronology of the area, with finds from the Chalcolithic period (3000 BC) right through to the Byzantine (13th century AD). Room 3, with its stone sarcophagi and Roman sculptures, is perhaps the most memorable.

Katopaphos

Most of the major sights in the Paphos region are in the harbour area of Katopaphos – including the Archaeological Park with its Roman mosaics, the Tombs of the Kings and the castle – but there are also a few surprising sights you might not ordinarily see.

Climb up inside the castle.

Small as it may be, pretty **Paphos Castle** (www.visitpafos.org.cy/Medieval_Castle_of_Paphos.aspx) is something of a symbol for the town. It's always worth a visit, if only to climb up, see the views, take a photo of the harbour – and put yourself firmly in holiday mode.

The castle might look like a stand-alone building, but in fact, the original tower here was just one of two built by the Lusignans in the 13th century; the Venetians pulled them down, and it was the Ottoman Turks who rebuilt the castle as you see it today.

Marvel at the Paphos mosaics ...

You'd be mad to holiday in Paphos without visiting the **Archaeological Park** (www.visitpafos.org.cy/Archaeological

_Park.aspx) – famous for its series of Roman floor mosaics. In the 3rd-century villa known as the **House of Dionysos**, for example, darkness lurks amid the classical scenes depicted in the mosaics: Dionysos, god of wine, presents wine to Akme, daughter of ill-fated Ikaros; Zeus, as an eagle, abducts Ganymede; Apollo reclines next to Daphne even as she turns into a tree; doomed lovers Pyramos and Thisbe are seen near the start of their tale; and the two "first wine drinkers" look decidedly the worse for wear.

Almost as fascinating is the **House of Theseus**, whose main feature is a labyrinth mosaic, at the heart of which Theseus slays the Minotaur.

... but save time for Saranta Kolones.

Though the mosaics might be the stars of the show, the medieval ruins known as **Saranta Kolones** – "40 columns" in Greek – are the cameo act. Here, in the corner of the Archaeological Park behind the car park, is the site of a 12th-century Lusignan castle which, at the time of its construction, overlooked Paphos harbour – but was destroyed in 1222 by a massive earthquake that redrew the shoreline. These days it offers some aesthetically pleasing arches and a good photo opportunity.

See tombs fit for kings.

You can have enormous fun clambering up and down (or rather, down and up) the ruins of the ancient necropolis known as the **Tombs of the Kings** (+357 26 306295, www.visitpafos.org.cy/Tombs_of_the_Kings.aspx), with its tombs going back as far as the 4th century BC. The grandeur of some of the tombs almost defies belief – one, supported by fluted Doric columns, seems to imitate the courtyard of a palace – though no "kings", in fact, were buried in any part of the site, despite the name.

Just one warning: if you visit in the summer heat and don't bring enough water, you could find the Tombs a bit of a slog, because the necropolis is built on a strung-out site.

If you want a meal on the harbour, try Ta Bania.

My tip for a sit-down *souvlaki* lunch on Paphos harbour is **Ta Bania** (+357 26 941558), a neat and tidy place on the seafront, done up in a sort of nautical art deco style. It's right round on the opposite side of the harbour from the castle, which means it isn't overly touristy – but you still get great views across the bay, and the food is pretty good too.

"Ta Bania", by the way, means "the baths" – and it's the name given to this area because there's a little concrete bathing spot here, with a seawater pool.

For caves and folklore, wander over Fabrika Hill.

Just inland of the Ayia Solomoni catacomb, on the road between the Tombs of the Kings Road crossroads and Katopaphos harbour, there are some interesting rock-cut caves which are easy to miss. These caves, evidence apparently of Hellenistic-era quarrying, are cut into Fabrika Hill – and it's possible to walk through them, climb up some rock-cut steps and emerge, blinking, into the sunlight of the hill above.

In Cypriot lore, this hill was known as the **Palace of Rigaina** – a word derived from the Latin *Regina*, referring to a "Queen" who supposedly lived here. It is said that this Queen agreed to marry the Byzantine hero Dighenis, if he could bring water to the site; he did so, but she broke her promise, upon which he threw a rock at her. The rock just north of the hill is still known as the Rock of Dighenis.

The little nearby grotto of **Ayia Solomoni** (www.visitpafos.org.cy/Agia_Solomoni_Church.aspx) is a bit more on the tourist trail and can easily be visited at the same time.

Visit Ayia Kyriaki church.

Without doubt the most beautiful church in Paphos is, ironically enough, no longer used by the Orthodox population of the town – and is instead shared by the Catholic and Anglican communities, for whom it is well known as a location for Cyprus weddings. This church, **Ayia Kyriaki**, is also known as Panayia Chrysopolitissa (Our Lady of the Golden City) and is sited right next to **St Paul's Pillar**, supposedly the spot where St Paul was tied and whipped for preaching Christianity.

Inside, the church's cruciform shape and huge dome are as dramatic as it gets. For service times or to arrange a wedding, check with either the Anglican community (www.paphosanglicanchurch.org.cy) or the Catholic (www.stpauls-catholic-parish-paphos.com).

Visit Sodap beach.

Yes, yes, it's not much of a secret – the main Paphos municipal beach (www.visitpafos.org.cy/Vrysoudia_beach_A.aspx), in and among the hotels, is well known among locals and tourists alike. Known as **Sodap beach** by the locals (after an old wine factory), it's an average strip of sand behind a big breakwater, not far from the heart of the city centre – but that's exactly what gives it its charm.

What's great about this place is the people it attracts – from the retired Cypriots and expats who come here for their early morning dip in winter, to chilled-out tourists who don't feel the need to head out to the bigger beach up at Coral Bay. Despite being undersized, it never seems to get overcrowded. Best of all, it's got a nice little cafe, the **Deck Bar**, where you can drink frappe (iced instant coffee) and while away the hours.

For Greek-style nightlife, try Metaxi Mas.

To experience local Greek cafe culture and nightlife in Paphos, head to the series of streets just north-east of the Almyra hotel. Here you'll find cafes aimed at younger Cypriots, such as **Metaxi Mas** – literally, "among ourselves" – at Diagorou 1. If you're staying in Paphos, this is a nicer place to go out than "bar street", the row of tourist bars a few streets west.

In September, go to the opera at Paphos Castle.

Each year as part of the **Pafos Aphrodite Festival** (www.pafc.com.cy), a different international opera company comes to Paphos – and hosts an opera with Paphos Castle as its backdrop. The performances are top-notch, but can continue long into the night – thanks partly to the long intervals, and partly to the long speeches given by local dignitaries; bring a cushion, perhaps.

Along the west coast: Coral Bay and beyond

In recent years the villages north of Paphos – notably Chlorakas, Emba and Peyia – have been heavily developed, and are home to a large British community; and the resort of Coral Bay, with its sandy beach, has become a full-blown villasville. But there is still beauty to be found – and further north still, the landscape turns wild, with dirt tracks leading to isolated beaches.

Visit the Mavrokolympos Dam.

A steep drive east into the hills from the Coral Bay road takes you up to the **Mavrokolympos Dam** – a world away from the bustle of the coast. It's all about the drive, really, but in the valley floor below the dam, you can just about see traces of an old, possibly Ottoman, aqueduct. East of the dam is a network of trails used by offroading enthusiasts.

Browse for pottery at Lemba.

If you're looking for unusual, traditional-style pottery, seek out **Lemba Pottery** (+357 26 270822, www.lembapottery .com) in the village of Lemba (official spelling: Lempa). It's good for gifts that nod to an ancient Greek aesthetic – such as jugs, goblets and water urns.

Escape the Coral Bay crowds at Maa.

If you're up at Coral Bay and fancy a bit of peace, it's worth visiting the Bronze Age site known as the **Palaeokastro** or "old castle" at Maa (www.visitpafos.org.cy/Maa_Paleokastro.aspx) – first populated more than 3,000 years ago by Mycenaean Greeks. It's not exactly Mycenae, and there isn't a great deal to see apart from some huge, fortified walls – but it's a fine place to get away from it all as you stand on the headland looking out to sea.

Visit Ayios Yeoryios near Peyia.

Right on the coast north-west of Peyia is the tiny, romantic little Greek Orthodox church of **Ayios Yeoryios**. It couldn't be in a better location – and if you come here late in the afternoon, the low sun simply floods the black and white tiled floor with light. There are also the ruins of two mosaic basilicas here – and it's possible to stop at a cafe overlooking the sea. The sunset, by the way, is something else – and that goes for the whole of this west-facing coast.

Enjoy the atmosphere at Viklari.

I couldn't possibly give an unbiased review of the **Viklari** taverna, because it's run by a distant (by non-Cypriot standards) cousin – but all I'll say is: if you like the idea of a place serving simple *souvla* (barbecued chunks of meat) on stone tables, on a shaded balcony looking out at some of the finest views in Cyprus, try it out. To get here, head up the coast road in the direction of Lara bay; the restaurant is slightly inland, right at the entrance to Avakas Gorge.

Walk the Avakas Gorge.

Avakas Gorge (www.islebright.com/links/250cy/017)[2] is a beauty spot almost unique in Cyprus. Here, you can enjoy an easy stroll or strenuous walk, depending on how far you decide to walk into the gorge – which begins as an enclosed delta, fertile with junipers and other evergreens, before narrowing through huge "gates" to the gorge proper, where high cliff walls are scarcely more than a few metres apart. Once inside, the path heads up stone-cut stairs and starts to criss-cross the riverbed – and the further upstream you go, the harder going the walk becomes. Upriver, it's possible to connect with a network of dirt tracks connecting to Pano or Kato Arodes – though for wayfinding beyond the gorge, you'd need to arm yourself with a printout of a satellite map.

Bear in mind that if there's any chance of rainfall on high ground, you might want to reconsider your plans; it can rain extremely heavily in Cyprus and flash flooding is a risk. Rockfalls, too, are a danger. In any case, you should take plenty of water and wear good boots!

See the turtles at Lara.

Lara Bay is in the middle of nowhere, which is good news for lovers of solitude – and very good news for the Mediterranean green turtles who nest here, given the threat to turtle nesting sites posed by tourist development. To get here, continue north on the coast road past Avakas Gorge, along an unmade road – it's far easier in a 4x4, but hardy types will probably find it ok in a two-wheel-drive. Be aware that there is little or no shade at Lara, but bringing an umbrella is a no-no because of turtle nesting sites – as, of course, is driving your car on to the beach.

For obvious reasons, Lara Bay – along with other beaches within the auspices of the Cyprus Turtle

Conservation Project – is closed at night in summer. However, visitors are still welcome during the day – and from July 20 or so onwards, it may be possible to see turtle hatchlings.

The Laona villages

The upland expanse of countryside between Peyia and Polis is one of the most beautiful areas in Cyprus, with some interesting villages and a generally slow pace of life. Not many people stop, but it's worth making the effort to do so.

Take the road less travelled.
The main Paphos-Polis road is an important road linking the city of Paphos to the beaches of the north-west – but can be a bit of a trial to negotiate, with all the heavy traffic, slow lorries, tailgaters and the like. So if you're going north from Paphos, consider heading out along the **old road** passing through the Laona district. The villages in these parts – Kathikas, Arodes (home of my great grandmother), Kritou Tera, Drouseia and Ineia – all reward a slow pace of tourism, and Kathikas has a few restaurants that are worth stopping in for lunch. There are agrotourism places to stay all over these parts – browse them at Cyprus Agrotourism (www.agrotourism.com.cy).

Pause at Ayia Aikaterini, Kritou Tera.
The little 15th-century church of **Ayia Aikaterini** (St Catherine) is just off the main Paphos-Polis road, but also

accessible via the old road if you drive down from Kritou Tera. Its three small domes give it a quirky, offbeat look – and it is also associated with a bizarre legend or two.

In one version of the story, the Byzantine border guard Dighenis wants to marry St Catherine, and she asks him to bring water to the site; when he does so, she escapes to sea and ultimately to Mount Sinai, even as Dighenis is hurling rocks into the sea after her. The story, which is still told in Kritou Tera, appears to associate St Catherine with Rigaina, the nebulous "queen" of Cyprus who appears in various Cypriot folk tales.

Go rock climbing.

The first thing I think of when I think of rock climbing in Cyprus is: "What about the snakes?" But if you're rather more fearless than me – and let's face it, most climbers must be – there's a website called **CyprusRocks** (www.cyprusrocks.eu; incidentally, it does) devoted to the sport and the art. The area near the villages of Drouseia and Ineia features fairly heavily, which adds another reason to visit this region.

Relax at Paradisos Hills.

East of the main Paphos-Polis road, in the village of Lysos, is a good, family-run hotel, **Paradisos Hills** (www.paradisoshills.com). It offers a good base for a tour of the Paphos Forest (see page 56) – but is also striking distance from Polis and the sea. I've stayed a night here, and the welcome is friendly, the location and views second to none, and the rooms are of a good standard and clean.

Along the south coast: east to Aphrodite's Rock

When the ancient Greeks spoke of "Paphos", they meant what we now call Palaipaphos ("old Paphos") – a settlement founded as early as 3900 BC, in and around the present-day village of Kouklia, about 15km east of the modern city. This area was the centre of the Aphrodite cult in antiquity – and remained so even after the Johnny-come-lately settlement at Nea Paphos ("new Paphos") was founded in the mere 4th century BC.

Spare time for Palaipaphos and Kouklia.

As the focal point of the Aphrodite cult for so many centuries, **Palaipaphos** (+357 26 432155, www.visitpafos.org.cy/Palaipafos_Museum.aspx) should be high on anyone's to-do list. This, after all, is where a fertility goddess was venerated – only latterly as Aphrodite – from as early as 3900 BC until nearly 400 AD. And while the sanctuary of Aphrodite itself can be difficult to get a sense of, there is enough in and near the site to capture the attention – including **La Cavocle**, a restored Frankish manor house hosting local finds, and, just outside the grounds, the 12th-century church of **Panayia Katholiki**.

After your visit to Palaipaphos, a good lunch stop is the welcoming **Efraim Ouzeri-Taverna** (+357 26 432082), right on the main square in Kouklia. To be honest, though, anywhere that styles itself as an *ouzeri* (place where ouzo is served, with titbits on the side) usually gets my vote.

Don’t miss Aphrodite’s Rock.

There are often too many visitors at **Aphrodite’s Rock**, famous as the supposed birthplace of Aphrodite – but that doesn’t mean it isn’t worth visiting, because it’s a genuinely beautiful place. The trick is to get here early in the morning when there’s hardly anyone else around – or even better, come before dawn and catch a sunrise. Watching here as the sea turns from a pastel grey to light turquoise, then suddenly fills with colour, is a magical experience.

There is more than one myth associated with the rock. In Greek, it’s known as Petra tou Romiou, or “Rock of the Greek” – the Greek in this instance being the Byzantine epic hero Dighenis, who threw the rock here, supposedly to ward off a Saracen raid. (Dighenis was an inveterate rock-hurler: as already mentioned, he also supposedly threw the rock at Fabrika Hill – see page 14.)

In recent years, tourists have taken to making little hearts out of the shingle on the stone, with lovers’ initials inside – a quaint little Aphrodite tradition in the making.

Get married at Vasilias Nikoklis.

Vasilias Nikoklis (+357 26 432211, www.vasilias.nikoklis.com), in Nikokleia, is a bit of a rarity: an agro-tourism venue that operates as a hotel, not a self-catering villa. Like many agrotourism places, it’s not luxurious, but it is situated magnificently, off a road that rises from the coast to the Troodos mountains – and is therefore a good base for both town and country. It’s also a romantic destination for wedding ceremonies and receptions – very different from the usual, beach-style Cypriot weddings.

Take a hike to an abandoned village by a lake...

The hills and valleys near Kouklia offer the chance to explore a couple of Cyprus' many abandoned villages – whether on foot, with a mountain bike, or by 4x4. One such village, **Phoinikas**, occupies a dramatic location, seeming to teeter right on the edge of the Asprokremmos reservoir. According to the PRIO Cyprus Centre (www.prio-cyprus-displacement.net), it's abandoned because its Turkish Cypriot population fled in the aftermath of the Turkish invasion in 1974.

Dirt tracks lead to Phoinikas from Nata and Anarita, but can be impassable after rain, so take extreme care and be ready to turn back before it gets too rough for your vehicle; the track from Anarita was very poor in spring 2012 after heavy winter rains, and not passable in an ordinary car, though it was possible to walk ahead for a sight of the village far below.

... or an abandoned village in a valley.

Another deserted village, **Kato Archimandrita**, is easier to reach: it's not far south of its sister village, Pano Archimandrita (www.archimandrita.org), where the villagers went when they abandoned the lower village in 1962. The reasons this time were the isolation and lack of infrastructure – but there's no lack of beauty or atmosphere, even though it's just a dirt track leading past the ruins of the old stone houses.

Passing through Pano Archimandrita, there's also an interesting old rock-carved church, the **Chapel of the 318 Fathers** – which, on my last visit a few years ago, had a resident snake in the hole above the door.

If you're off in search of an abandoned village anywhere in Cyprus, by the way, it's a good idea to bring a printout of a satellite map.

Wait for a plane at Yeroskipou beach.

On Rikkos Beach, Yeroskipou, is the modern **Seaside Cafe** (+357 99 629568), that's good for killing time while you're waiting for your Paphos flight – all the while watching planes as they climb westward toward Britain and Europe. Be warned, though: the departure terminal is still around 15 minutes' drive from here, as you have to head back to the B6 road (the old Paphos-Limassol road) to get there.

If even the Seaside Cafe seems a bit far from the airport, then there are a few places to swim and drink coffee at **Timi Beach**, just off the airport loop road. Just follow any of the tracks leading south from the airport road (but watch out for overtaking taxis as you do).

Into the hills: up to Pano Panayia

A fantastic day out from Paphos is to make a circular tour via Pano Panayia – a route which takes you past wineries, monasteries and fine Cypriot landscapes.

Explore the hermitage of Ayios Neophytos.

The monastery of **Ayios Neophytos** (www.visitpafos.org.cy/Saint_Neophytos_Monastery.aspx) is firmly on the tourist trail – but no less worth exploring for that. Here is the cave where, in the 12th century, the hermit Neophytos carved his sanctuary or *enkleistra* out of the rock – and then built another, higher up, to try to seclude himself from the monks who followed him. Come here to clamber up into the rock-cut caves and see some fine Byzantine frescoes.

Have coffee at Houlou, home of Arodafnousa.

The village of **Houlou** (official spelling: Choulou) is on the slow road up to Panayia – but it's worth coming up this way because of an interesting story associated with the village. Here – according to the salacious account published a century later by the monk Leontios Machairas – was where Peter I, the 14th-century Lusignan king of Cyprus, kept his pregnant mistress Joanna, widow of a local lord; thereby enraging his wife, Eleanor of Aragon. According to Machairas, Eleanor captured Joanna while Peter was away – and after unsuccessfully trying to force an abortion via narcotic and physical means (including grinding a pestle and mortar on its mother's belly) she then ordered the infant to be brought to her on its birth, after which it was never heard of again.

The story is retold in a traditional Cypriot poem, which recasts the mistress as a village girl called Arodafnousa; in this version Arodafnousa, the youngest and most beautiful of three sisters, is murdered by the jealous queen.

Visit the monastery at Chrysoroyiatissa.

Very few monasteries in the world are called "Our Lady of the Golden Pomegranate", as this one is – but that's by no means the only reason to visit **Chrysoroyiatissa** (+357 26 722457, www.islebright.com/links/250cy/027; alternative spellings many and various), just a few miles south of Pano Panayia. It's one of the most atmospheric monasteries in Cyprus, enjoying great views down into the valley below, and a relaxed feel among its Norman-inspired arches. The monks at Chrysoroyiatissa also make an easy-drinking red wine, Ayios Elias, which can be found in most Cypriot supermarkets (and you don't even need to read "Chrysoroyiatissa" in Greek to find it).

Go wine-tasting at Kolios.

The sheer number of wineries in these villages is bewildering – but if you have to go to one, you could do worse than the stone-built **Kolios winery** (+357 26 724090) at Statos Ayios-Photios. The winery is best known for producing Persefoni, a light-drinking white wine from the Cypriot *xynisteri* grape – and if you stop here, you can taste wines in the cellar and, of course, buy a bottle or two if you wish. With a day's notice, the folks at Kolios will prepare a *meze* at around €20 a head with free wine – which you can enjoy in their terrace dining room, which boasts 180-degree views of the valley to the west. Groups of expats and locals alike can be found here, availing themselves of the deal.

Other wineries on the way up to Panayia include **Vouni Panayia** (+357 26 722770, www.vounipanayiawinery.com), near Chrysoroyiatissa, with a grand vista over the Asproyia dam; **Tsangarides winery** (+357 26 722777, www.tsangarideswinery.com) in Lemona, not far from Houlou; the **Ezousa winery** (+357 7000 8844) near the new

Kannaviou dam; and of course the Chrysoroyiatissa monastery itself.[4]

Detour to the monastery of Panayia tou Sinti.

For isolated beauty, it's hard to beat **Panayia tou Sinti**, a restored, 16th-century monastery on the banks of a river valley in an unpopulated part of Cyprus. To get there, you follow a winding, 5km-long, partly metalled road from Pentalia – passable in a two-wheel drive, but more fun on a mountain bike or by 4x4 – until at last you see the church, with its octagonal dome and neat little courtyard, sitting squat among the fields (and polytunnels) below you. Wandering around the church, you'll probably be alone bar the nearby farmers – and you'll have time to appreciate a restoration that won a Europa Nostra award when it was completed.

There are alternative routes to Panayia tou Sinti. First, it's possible to get there by walking along the Xeros Potamos valley from the Roudias Venetian bridge, as outlined by Phivos Ioannides on **Cyprus Walks Etc** (www.cypruswalksetc.com; Ioannides also arranges scheduled tours of the valley and other parts of Cyprus). Second, when you reach the church, a track signs you on to the village of Salamiou, so it seems possible to get there from the eastern side of the valley.

Follow the Venetian bridges nature trail.

The Venetians built several bridges in this part of Cyprus – and a fascinating, 17km-long **nature trail** connects three of them: the Elias (Elia), Tzelephos (Kelefos) and Routhkias

(Roudia) bridges. It's a linear walk, so you'd need transport at one end.

The most impressive of the bridges is the Tzelephos bridge, whose arch reaches gracefully across a riverbed amid a forest.

For something a little bit different, meanwhile, the horse-riding company **Ride in Cyprus** (www.rideincyprus.com) offers a trek on horseback along the "Venetian camel trail" taking in all three of the bridges.

Consider staying in Panayia.

If you like a slow pace of life, you could do worse than stay a day or two in **Pano Panayia**. There are no fewer than five agrotourism properties (www.agrotourism.com.cy) in the village itself, not to mention a network of nature trails through the vineyards to keep you busy – so a day or two spent at altitude here makes a refreshing change from life on the coast.

Panayia also makes a convenient stopover point if you plan to make the long drive into the Paphos Forest and Tillyria, toward the moufflon enclosure at Stavros tis Psokas (see page 56).

Along the north coast: Akamas to Morphou bay

The Akamas peninsula is one of the undisputed beauty spots of Cyprus – a nature reserve known for its wildflowers and sea views. The peninsula protects the western half of Chrysochou Bay from the prevailing winds. Heading north and east, the coast becomes more isolated as it sweeps up toward Kato Pyrgos at the start of Morphou Bay.

Walk the Aphrodite trail

Lots of people drive up to the oversold Baths of Aphrodite, at the entrance to the Akamas peninsula – but not as many go on to walk the excellent nature trails of the peninsula. Which is a shame, because in spring in particular, an **Akamas walk** is worth arranging your entire holiday around. If you think of Cyprus as just a dry, dusty place, come here at this time of year and you'll be disabused of the idea: the Akamas in March is often covered with wildflowers – from carpets of poppies to exotic orchids to rock roses dotted in the scrub.

The shortest and most accessible of the trails is the **Aphrodite trail**, which offers views down into Chrysochou Bay – not to mention the odd encounter with a herd of goats. For an overview, pick up a leaflet from a tourist office.

Swim in the Blue Lagoon

On a quest for the best place to swim in Cyprus? The tiny **Blue Lagoon**, on a protected stretch of coast near the north-west tip of the island, should go on your list. This isolated spot, accessible only by dirt track or by sea, is a dreamy little cove where you can snorkel among shoals of fish in a crystal-clear sea. When the sea is calm – and if anywhere will be calm, it will be the Blue Lagoon – it's idyllic.

Part of the fun of swimming at the Blue Lagoon is the

effort it takes to get there. You either go by boat from the fishing harbour at Latchi, or you head along the dirt track from the Baths of Aphrodite for about two miles along the north coast, which you can do on foot, by mountain bike, or by 4x4. The Blue Lagoon is the one next to a tiny islet, just offshore.

Further up the coast from the Blue Lagoon is **Fontana Amorosa**, another idyllic sandy bay.

For sheer luxury, stay at the Anassa.

If you can afford it, that is. Located in an idyllic, north-facing corner of the island, right next to the Akamas peninsula, the **Anassa hotel** (+357 26 888000, www.anassa.com.cy) is the ideal place to enjoy a romantic, luxurious break – but prices are, unsurprisingly, high.

Drive east to Kato Pyrgos

Some people will go a long way to get away from it all – and if you love remoteness, you'll love the village of **Kato Pyrgos** (www.katopyrgos.org). With sea to the north, the Green Line to the east, the Troodos mountains to the south and a long, circuitous access road around the Kokkina exclave to the west, it's a village that demands serious effort to reach. When you get there, you might be surprised to find that it's quite a sizeable resort, but it has a family-friendly feel – and there are little beaches and tavernas dotted along the sweep of Chrysochou Bay.

Since 2010, the Limnitis crossing has opened, meaning that it's now also possible to cross the Green Line near Kato Pyrgos and, after a fairly short drive, visit the ancient palace of Vouni (see page 122). The crossing is also useful for residents of Kato Pyrgos, who can now visit Nicosia without having to make the long detour via Paphos.

2. Things to do in Limassol

Limassol (Greek: Lemesos) is a big, fast-growing holiday town with good nightlife and nightmare traffic – but the area around the city has much to offer besides urban pleasures. West of Limassol is the Sovereign Base Area of Akrotiri (western SBA), part of the British Overseas Territory on the island[5] – boasting top-drawer sights such as Curium and Kolossi Castle, not to mention wild beaches and the salt lake of Akrotiri. Further west still, Pissouri is a genteel resort which makes a brilliant base for a holiday. Heading north into the hills, you'll find handsome old wine villages waiting to be explored.

In the city: Limassol

Trendy hotels, decent nightlife, respectable beaches and a thriving arts scene make Limassol great for the young at heart. But it's a nightmare of a city to drive in, with little public transport, confusing roads and unruly traffic. Most upmarket hotels – with the exception of the renovated

Londa, which is more central – are east of the city, with a seafront bus or taxi needed to get you into town.

Do the tour of Limassol Castle.

It might not be much of a fortress – but **Limassol Castle** (+357 25 305419, www.islebright.com/links/250cy/043) is worth visiting, both for its history and for the cobblestone streets of bars, cafes and shops that surround it. First the history: this was where the crusading Richard I of England supposedly married Berengaria of Navarre in 1191 – just after making war on the tyrant Isaac and conquering the island. As for the atmosphere: once done with the castle, take a tour of the cobbled streets around it, have a coffee, then look in on the Evagoras Lanitis Centre (www.lanitisfoundation.org/?page_id=883) at the west of the square, which hosts some heavyweight exhibitions.

You may also wish to look in at the little unnamed shop owned by Paris Panayi, between the Bellini and Fourno cafes – here you can find the "Mellona" brand of flavoured honey, including carob-infused honey, a fine Cypriot souvenir for culinary types.

Eat at Ta Piatakia.

If you've never had a salad with *kefalotiri* (hard goat's cheese) and fresh spring strawberries in it, get yourself along to **Ta Piatakia** (+357 25 745017, www.tapiatakia.com) and see what you've been missing. Ta Piatakia ("Little Plates") is the kind of restaurant that Cyprus could do with more of: a place that offers a modern twist on traditional Cypriot cooking.

The layout of the restaurant also encourages you to spend money on wine – and why not?

Discover the art scene.

Unsurprisingly given the social changes Limassol has seen over the past 30 years, the city has a thriving arts scene. **Theatro Ena**, in the old art deco municipal market just east of the castle area, is a major focus for theatre and arts installations – while the **Rialto Theatre** (www.rialto .com.cy), several streets back from the seafront on Plateia Iroon (Heroes' Square), hosts several arts festivals including "Cyprus Rialto Ethnic", a world music festival that debuted in summer 2011.

Unwind at KafeNey.

Laid-back, intimate, jazzy and eastern – that sums up the sound of **KafeNey** (www.facebook.com/kafeney), an unpretentious venue for live music that also doubles as a pretty cool cafe-bar, around the corner from the city's Turkish baths. For just a drink, this is a great little bolthole, kitted out simply with village chairs and mosaic tables, while the menu – beer, wine, *zivaneia*, *frappe*, Cyprus coffee, ice tea or juice – is simplicity itself. It's also possible to buy CDs by Cypriot guitarist and composer Savvas Houvartas, a member of the KafeNey house band.

Quite near KafeNey, meanwhile, is an alley known as Zik Zak (Cypriot for "zig zag"), with a couple of interesting places on it including **Chouzouri**, a trendy cafe-bar, and next door the **Zen Art Studio Gallery**, which sells modern, spirituality-inspired artwork.

Buy a memento of Cyprus at Thesis.

On the face of it, **Thesis** (+357 25 369479, www.thesisinteriors.blogspot.co.uk) – run by the same team as Apokryfo, the luxury "traditional houses" in Lophou (page 50) – is a decent, modern furniture shop with a traditional Cypriot twist. But cleverly, the company also stocks smaller pieces that encourage tourists to spend money, such as occasional plates and picture frames, often designed by local artists; and there's also a little cafe, Antithesis, next door. It's well worth a browse – and there's a branch in Larnaca, too.

Drop in at the Mosaic Collective.

Almost opposite Thesis on Ayiou Andrea is the **Mosaic Collective** (+357 25 348051, www.mosaic-collective.net), where you can buy mosaics and mosaic-making equipment, or even arrange to have mosaic-making lessons while you're on holiday.

Wander around the Turkish quarter.

It's easy to spot the old **Turkish district** of Limassol by looking at a map – the street names such as "Ankara" and "Gazi Pasa" give the game away. It's a run-down area these days, but landmarks include the minarets of the Cami Cabir and Cami Jedid mosques, and Ottoman-style covered balconies, many now fallen into disrepair.

For a boutique hotel, stay at the Londa.

If you're looking for an upmarket hotel that's smaller and more central than most of the tourist hotels, the **Londa**

(+357 25 865555, www.londahotel.com) is a sound choice. On the outside it looks like a 1970s apartment block, but inside it's modern, elegant and comfortable; though it's slightly let down by its small beach.

Celebrate Carnival season.

Carnival in Cyprus isn't as crazy as in Spain or Latin America, but if you're on the island during the season (February or March) and in the mood for a party, you should go to Limassol and let your hair down. There are parades, fireworks and also appearances by serenaders.

During Carnival season, don't miss **Tsiknopempti** or "Smoky Thursday" when people set their barbecues up in the streets to grill meat in the open air. Tsiknopempti is 10 days before the start of Greek Orthodox Lent.

Taste Cyprus at the Limassol Wine Festival – and other festivals besides.

With the weather cooling after the excessive summer heat, mid-September onwards is festival season in Cyprus. In Limassol, this is the month of the **Limassol Wine Festival** – a three-day outdoor festival in the Limassol municipal gardens, near the seafront, where you can try and buy wines from all over the island.

Near Limassol, there are also autumn grape festivals in many of the Troodos villages, celebrating the production of wine byproducts such as the sweet *palouzes* and the firewater *zivaneia*; the *pastelli* (carob-sweet) festival in Anoyira (see page 43); and also the festival of Apostolos Andreas in Pissouri (see page 42).

Along the coast: the western SBA

Much of the coastline west of Limassol is British soil: from Avdimou Bay to just outside the port of Limassol, and some way inland, you're inside the Sovereign Base Area of Akrotiri.[5] Happily for nature-lovers, this stretch of coast is – thanks to the terms of the agreement under which Britain retained its bases – some of the least developed in Cyprus.

If nothing else, drive the old main road.
From Episkopi onwards, the **old road** from Limassol towards Paphos – shown on maps as the B6 – is a delight. Using this road, you can drive past the ancient Curium archaeological site (and Curium Beach); twist up and down through scenic Happy Valley, not only home to British military sports pitches but also griffon vultures and other migratory birds; then head on past the clifftop village of Pissouri toward Aphrodite's Rock. Yes, the motorway will get you there faster, but for sheer joy, no functional highway could ever compete.

Make time for all the sites at Curium.
The Roman mosaics and amphitheatre at **Curium** (+357 25 934250, www.islebright.com/links/250cy/052; known in Greek as "Kourion") are, of course, the big draw in this part of Cyprus – and it's tempting just to make a quick tour of these archaeological wonders and then head down for lunch on the beach (and if you do this, I would recommend **Chris**

Blue Beach for its fish and chips). Yet there is more to see. The **Sanctuary of Apollo Hylates**, just off the B6, is one of the best sites in Cyprus – evoking as it does the worship of woodland gods and nymphs, it's atmospheric if you visit in spring. Nearby is a restored **stadium**, free to enter and a good place (outside the heat of summer) for a bit of a runaround to test your pace.

But perhaps the least visited attraction is the most extraordinary: the **Curium Museum** (+357 25 932453, www.islebright.com/links/250cy/053), hidden away in the back streets of the nearby village of Episkopi. Here the most poignant find on display is the preserved skeletons of a man, woman and child killed in an earthquake in the 4th century. Their bodies were found in the foetal position – buried as they sheltered from the violence of the quake.

Watch a Shakespeare play at Curium.

Towards the end of June each year, the ancient theatre at Curium plays host not to ancient Greek drama as you might expect, but to Shakespeare. The performances are organised by local groups. Find out more by visiting the **Shakespeare at Curium** group on Facebook – and when you come, bring a cushion.

Buy springtime strawberries on the way to Curium Beach.

One last thing to say about Curium: if you visit in spring, stop off by the little **strawberry stall** on the way down to Curium Beach – on the left side of the road as you head toward the sea – for a seasonal treat.

See the sugar mill next to Kolossi Castle.

Kolossi Castle (+357 25 934907) is on everyone's tourist itinerary, and rightly so – although only a small fortress, it's well known as the commanderie of the Knights of St John, who not only ruled Cyprus for centuries but made the island famous for its *commandaria*, the red sweet wine that's thought to be the oldest named wine in the world. The existing keep was built in the mid-15th century.

When you're done with the castle, take a peek at the 14th-century **sugar factory** and **sugar mill**, on the eastern edge of the site. The mill bears testament to Cyprus' global importance as a sugar exporter for centuries – a trade from which the knights profited handsomely.

Nearby is the little church of **Ayios Evstathios**, a three-aisled Byzantine construction, restored in the 15th century and thought to be a chapel used by the knights.

Get away from it all at Avdimou Bay...

The coast at **Avdimou Bay** is among the wildest and most windswept in the whole of Cyprus – and still worth a stop. To reach the sea, follow the road south from the Avdimou motorway exit; heading into British territory, you continue down a single-track road past some vineyards (and ancient tombs), which opens out at the bottom at a long beach that's perfect for romantic walks by the sea. Here, from spring to autumn, the **Kyrenia Beach Cafe** serves reliable Cypriot classics along with British favourites such as pies.

The wind here makes the conditions difficult for swimming, but is perfect for the many **kitesurfing** enthusiasts who come here; for more information on kitesurfing at Avdimou and nearby beaches, visit Kiteboarding Cyprus (www.kiteboardingcyprus.com) or Cyprus Wind (www.cyprus-wind.com).

... or try Melanda for swimming.

If you prefer to swim, not far from Avdimou Bay is another beach, **Melanda**, which is more sheltered and more popular, though perhaps not as romantic. Instead of heading directly south from the motorway junction, you go a short distance west toward Pissouri along the B6 (old road), then turn left at the sign for Melanda. There's a little harbour here, with the odd fishing boat, and an informal beach cafe with an interesting old relief map of Cyprus on the wall.

Spot flying visitors in Akrotiri.

Every winter, thousands of migratory flamingos make their home on the salt lake on the **Akrotiri peninsula**. It's never a good idea to take any vehicle close to the lake (even a 4x4), but if you take the little road from Akrotiri village toward Ayios Nikolaos monastery, you can get a decent view of the birds. While here, stop off at Ayios Nikolaos – the monastery is known as **Nicholas of the Cats**, because it was supposedly home to a huge community of cats who killed all the snakes in the area.

The far south of the peninsula is off-limits because it's an RAF base – but this does mean there's also another kind of flying visitor who, if you're lucky, you may get to see. The Red Arrows can occasionally be seen in the skies above Akrotiri in spring, practising displays – and, because of their huge vapour trails, can even be visible from high up in the hills if you happen to be looking in the right direction at the time.

Along the coast: Pissouri

If you prefer relaxed resorts to urban cool, Pissouri makes a fantastic base. The area is split between two communities: Pissouri village, perched up high on its own hill – with some goodish restaurants and a modern amphitheatre that hosts festivals in summer – and a couple of miles away, Pissouri Bay, the former fishing harbour, now a small but pleasant resort.

Live the high life at the Columbia Beach.

If you have the budget and you want a comfortable place to stay in Pissouri Bay, the **Columbia Beach Resort** (+357 25 833000, www.columbia-hotels.com/en/beach-resort-cyprus), or its cheaper sister hotel the **Columbia Beachotel** (+357 25 833333, www.columbia-hotels.com/en/beach-hotel-cyprus), are ideal choices. But you don't need to be a guest to enjoy an outdoor drink or even a spa treatment at the complex; prices aren't the cheapest, but I'd recommend you head down here of a late afternoon, to enjoy the high life by the irrigated lawns near the sea.

There is even an interesting bit of tourism you can do in the grounds of the Columbia Beach Resort. On the grass here is a tiny wedding chapel with the most extraordinary bright blue murals. It's like no other church in Cyprus – and it's worth poking your nose in while wandering around.

When in Pissouri Bay, eat at Limanaki.
There are plenty of good places to eat in Pissouri Bay, from traditional seaside tavernas to a curry house – but there's one restaurant that outshines the rest, and that's **Limanaki** (+357 25 221288, www. limanakipissouri.com). Offering the right blend of formality and informality, Limanaki is a place to eat a mix of Mediterranean and Asian-inspired dishes; though if you want to order the *meze*, you need to book in advance. Limanaki also runs a charity cookery school on Mondays.

Up at Pissouri village, pop into the Sparti Pub.
There may be more authentic places to relax in Pissouri Square, but for a quick drink, I have a soft spot for the **Sparti Pub** (+357 25 221772). It couldn't be more informal: scarcely more than a room facing out on to a little pedestrianised alleyway, with a few tables and some informal seating outside.

The Anoyira loop

Easily accessible on a loop from Pissouri, Anoyira (official spelling: "Anogyra"; www.anogyra.org) is a little village with a big reputation for friendliness and charm. Once upon a time it was a centre for carob production, and in the village there is a carob museum, a cafe-bar, agrotourism rooms and traditional barber's shop. In mid-September every year, there's also a festival to celebrate the production of *pastelli*, a kind of carob syrup paste.

I lived in this village – which explains the focus on this small area of Cyprus.

Visit the church of Timios Stavros.

Just on the right before you enter Anoyira, you'll see a sign for the little church of **Timios Stavros** – a half-restored cruciform church standing amid the ruins of the larger monastic complex it once was. It's a timeless place – and it's well worth opening up the doors at both front and back to let the light flood in and give you a sense of its beauty inside.

Look for the standing stone.

Also on the right as you approach the village, there is another little landmark worth seeing. It's inside the Greek Orthodox churchyard, where – among the gleaming white headstones – you'll find a curious **standing stone**; that is, a stone with a square hole in the middle of it.

Some Cypriots once believed that stones like this held mystical powers, and would pass their babies through the holes in an attempt to cure illnesses. Research, however, demonstrates that the stones were in fact parts of ancient olive presses – a prosaic truth which nevertheless offers a bit of a romance of its own.

Don't miss the mosque and Muslim graveyard.

It's easy to miss, but just as you enter the village itself, there's a little **mosque** without a minaret on the left hand side of the road – testament to the Turkish Cypriot community that once shared this mixed village. Even easier to miss is the **Muslim graveyard**, on the right side of the road on the way into the village, quite near the Greek churchyard – it's a field bound by a stone wall.

Try carobs and coffee.

If you're in Anoyira, you really shouldn't miss the **carob museum** – a rural museum project in the heart of the village. It's an opportunity to explore the history of *pastelli*, the traditional carob-based sweet celebrated in an annual village festival in September – and learn how carob was once such a major Cypriot export that it was known as "black gold". You can buy any number of carob products here including the *pastelli* itself and carob powder that can be used in place of cocoa; personally I am a fan of carob-flavoured honey.

After visiting the museum, repair to the coffee shop around the corner for a Cyprus coffee – or perhaps something stronger.

Go printmaking with Hambis.

Heading out of Anoyira, follow the back roads out of the village via the hamlet of Ayios Thomas to the village of Platanisteia – to find the **Hambis Printmaking Museum** (+357 25 222772, www.forthdesignstudio.com/hambis/hambis), a rural studio run by Hambis Tsangaris, one of Cyprus' best known artists. Here you can not only see a gallery of the artist's work, but get an introduction to the art of printmaking and even attend workshops in linocut, aquatint, screenprint and other crafts. The centre has close links with the village of Anoyira – and some of the workshops are based there.

Have dinner at Platanisteia.

If you're staying in Pissouri or Anoyira and on the lookout for an authentic village taverna, the **Plataniskeia Tavern** (+357 99 843941) – right opposite the printmaking museum – might just be what you're looking for. It's a pretty good place, serving traditionally Cypriot food in a stone house with an out-of-the-way feel. Ring ahead, though, to check if they're open, especially out of season.

According to the PRIO Cyprus Centre (www.prio-cyprus-displacement.net), which maps internal displacement in the island, Platanisteia was home to a large Turkish Cypriot community before 1974; after the invasion, they sought refuge in the Sovereign Base Areas and later made homes in the north.

Go for a walk up to the Hapotami valley.

Near Anoyira is a hidden area of natural beauty: the **Hapotami**, a steep-sided, fertile valley that narrows here to just a few hundred metres across. Along the ridge on the southern side runs a jeep track, offering fine views north-east up to the Troodos mountains and west to the Oreites wind farm.

To get here from Anoyira, walk due north up the steep little road leading away from the village square (which soon turns into a track); after about a mile's climb you'll find yourself up at the edge of the ridge. From here you could simply retrace your steps; or, to make a circle, turn left and keep the valley on your right for a short distance, before taking the first main track on the left to swing back down into Anoyira once more.

Try the Oleastro.

If you're interested in olives, an unusual attraction east of Anoyira is the **Oleastro** (www.oleastro.com.cy), an olive mill that's also a restaurant and exhibition space. It's a reasonable enough spot for a buffet lunch, and children are entertained by the water mill exhibition; it's also possible, if you're interested, to see many different labelled varieties of olive tree.

Into the hills: Omodos and around

The western Limassol wine villages or Krasohoria make up one of the most attractive regions in Cyprus, with no shortage of stone terraces on its steep, vine-covered slopes. Of the villages, Omodos is most geared up for tourism; it has a much-visited church and an excellent restaurant. But most of the villages in the area, in fact, are well worth a stop, not just the bigger ones listed here.

Eat at Stou Kyr Yianni, Omodos.

This is a great restaurant. Tucked away in a little alleyway in Omodos, **Stou Kyr Yianni** (+357 25 422100, www.omodosvillagecottage.com/rest.html; translation: At Mister Yianni's) offers food and drink that real Kyprophiles will love – from *trahana* soup to stuffed courgettes to home-made village wine. There's also some folky guitar music on a Saturday night and the opportunity to smoke a *shisha* if you so desire. Like many places in Cyprus, the restaurant has no menu – you just get the *meze*, and if you don't fancy something, you pass over it and have something else.

One of the very nicest things about the restaurant is that if you come here in the evening and park in the main Omodos car park, the route on foot to Stou Kyr Yianni takes you right through the heart of the village and even through the courtyard of the **Timios Stavros monastery**, a major sight in its own right.

One final tip: there are two parts to Stou Kyr Yianni, a modern indoor restaurant area and a romantic covered courtyard. In the summer months, the courtyard is the place to be, so try to ask for a table in this area when you reserve.

See the donkeys at Vouni...

Not far from Omodos, Vouni (Greek for "mountain") is a hill village of a similar size, but which hasn't undergone prettification in quite the same way. Not far from here is the **Vouni Donkey Sanctuary** (+357 25 945488, www.donkeysanctuarycyprus.org) – which provides shelter and quality veterinary care for some of the many Cypriot donkeys that find themselves in need of rescue. Admission is free, but donations are encouraged.

... and eat out.

In the village itself, there is a good restaurant, **I Oraia Ellas** (+357 25 944328), which concentrates on Greek (rather than Cypriot) food. The sign is in Greek script only, so brush up before you go – or just enjoy wandering the village streets among the stone houses, as you try to find the place.

Make glass mosaics in Malia.

The hill village of Malia, just off the Limassol-Omodos road, is home to **A Touch of Glass** (www.maliaglass.com) – a rural art business run by Sarah and Mary, two British expats, in their studio in a traditional village house. They specialise in either stained glass or glass mosaic, and it's possible to either buy their work (wrap it carefully!) or take part in a workshop. You're also walking distance from a village taverna where you can get lunch.

Try lunch with a view at Vasa.

For one of the best lunchtime views in Cyprus – and there are plenty on the list – seek out the village of Vasa Koilaniou, known locally as Vasa. Here, head up to **O Pyrgos** (+357 25 942655, www.pyrkostavern.com), which means "tower"; you can either eat out on the balcony or, in poor weather, retreat into the traditional interior.

Into the hills: the Commandaria region

The eastern edge of the Limassol wine region has long been devoted to *commandaria* – the red, sweet fortified wine that once made Cyprus famous. *Commandaria* brought prosperity to villages such as Lophou (Lofou) and Lania – as is clear from the huge numbers of houses that, with migration to the cities, began to fall into disrepair. Happily, some have now been revitalised as agrotourism accommodation and, particularly in and around Lania, retirement homes for a burgeoning expat community.

Stay in an agrotourism hotel, Lophou.

The grand old *commandaria* wine village of Lophou has the distinction of being home to two good agrotourism hotels, with confusingly similar names.

Apokryfo (+357 25 813777, www.apokryfo.com), the more upmarket of the two, is a collection of luxury rooms and cottages based around a central courtyard with a pool; the restaurant here, Agrino, offers an exceptionally good *meze* for around €35.

Cheaper accommodation is available at **Agrovino** (+357 25 470202, www.lofou-agrovino.com), which offers simpler studios in traditional style with a welcoming taverna of its own. Either would make a great base for a chilled-out break in the hills.

Have Sunday lunch at Lania.

At weekend lunchtimes, the **Lania Tavern** (+357 25 432398) is full of locals and expats enjoying a simple Cyprus *meze* on the shaded terrace – so it's well worth heading up to Lania to join them, then having a look into the local art galleries and traditional folk museum (open on Sundays).

Lania (also spelt Laneia) is a seriously lively place by Cyprus village standards, and there are regular art and music events arranged by the British expat and Greek Cypriot communities here; visit Cyprus Village Link (www.cyprusvillagelink.com) to know more.

Look into the church at Doros.
One of the most unusual churches in the area is the old church of **Ayios Epiphanios** in the village of Doros. Unlike the many cruciform, Byzantine churches in these parts, it's a simple rectangular structure with a wooden pitched roof – more typical of the Troodos style, and uncommon at this relatively low altitude.

Into the hills: Vikla and Akapnou

The area around Vikla and Akapnou, near the border with the Larnaca region, is little visited, little known and thoroughly interesting. Unfortunately, the road up via Parekklisia and Kellaki is overrun by heavy lorries heading down from a huge upland quarry, so demands care.

Play golf near the abandoned village of Vikla.
Even if you can't stand golf, it's worth visiting **Vikla**. It's hard to tell which is the more striking – the abandoned village on a hilltop, full of derelict houses, with the restored Greek Orthodox church of St John at its highest point; or the manicured greens on the plateau below, where expat Brits come to play golf in the back of beyond. The clubhouse here at **Vikla Golf** (www.vikla4golf.com) is informal, and a good place (indeed, the only place) to stop by for a quick drink.

To get here, it's a long and winding road from Kellaki – or if you're in a 4x4, there's a dirt track up from Akapnou.

Drink coffee at Akapnou.

Just down the dirt track north from Vikla, the restored village of **Akapnou** is well worth a visit, if only to have a morning coffee at the friendly post office cum coffee shop. According to local tradition, the Rigaina or semi-mythical "Queen" of Cyprus died not far from here after a battle with Saracen raiders, meeting her death as she escaped toward to Lefkara. To the west of the village there is a highly recommended Venetian-built bridge and, slightly further down the road to Eptagonia, an ancient-looking shrine.

3. Things to do in Troodos

The Troodos mountain range is the green heart of Cyprus – the place you go to get away from the heat and frenetic pace of the coast. It's a place of endless winding roads through pine forests – and villages boasting agrotourism accommodation, painted churches, traditional produce, top-notch wineries and tavernas with a view.

High Troodos

If you're thinking of climbing or driving to the highest peak of Cyprus, forget it – the peak of Mount Olympus is home to a military installation, one of the big white "golf balls" visible from most of the island. But there's plenty to do near the top – including, walk, ski, and even (on the right day of the year) visit a monastery that's usually closed.

The main hill stations of Troodos are the villages of Platres and Prodromos, both of which had their halcyon days in the 1930s, when King Farouk of Egypt would visit the area's then ultra-exclusive hotels, Forest Park in Platres (still going) and the Berengaria in Prodromos (sadly fallen into disrepair).

Go skiing on Mount Olympus.

The **ski** season in Cyprus is usually short, starting in January and in good years lasting into March. The most complicated thing may be getting there – if the weather has been bad, you may need snow chains on your car – but on arrival, things are informal and it's easy enough to get out on to the slopes for a bit of a potter. For novices, the best place to head is Sun Valley, where you can easily hire equipment and receive tuition. For prices, piste conditions and phone numbers for reservations, contact the Cyprus Ski Federation and Club (www.cyprusski.com) or SkiCyprus.com (www.skicyprus.com).

It can be tricky finding a suitably hearty meal after a morning's skiing on Mount Olympus, so it's a good idea to bring sandwiches with you. If you forget (as I did), then head north to the village of Prodromos – where **To Byzantion** (+357 25 463333) sometimes has a buffet going.

By the way, it is possible to ski in Troodos in the morning and swim in the sea in the afternoon, as the tourist brochures often suggest – but you probably wouldn't want to, as the sea in winter is usually pretty cold.

See Trooditissa on August 15.

Judging by older guidebooks, casual visitors used to be able to pay a visit to **Trooditissa monastery**, situated on the road between Platres and Prodromos that skirts Troodos to the west – but that's no longer the case. Happily, each year on

August 15, a festival is held in the grounds of the monastery to celebrate the Dormition of the Virgin Mary, so this is a chance not only to see a Greek Cypriot religious festival in full flow, but to take a look around.

Walk down to the Caledonia Falls, Platres...

One of the two classic walks in Troodos is the 3km downhill **Caledonia trail** (www.islebright.com/links/250cy/073) from Troodos to the Psilodendro trout farm near Platres, via the Caledonia Falls. The walk starts from near the presidential cottage on the winding road down from Troodos Square. Heading south, it roughly traces the path of the Kryos Potamos ("cold river") past the falls – before concluding at the Psilodendro ("tall tree") trout farm, where you can eat fresh trout for lunch before ordering a taxi back.

Alternatively, a tougher 5km path known as the **Pouziaris trail** (www.islebright.com/links/250cy/074) completes the loop.

...or skirt the Olympus peak.

The other classic walking trail in the high Troodos is the 7km, circular **Artemis trail** (www.islebright.com/links/250cy/075) which skirts the peak of Mount Olympus. The trail might be high in altitude, but it's mostly flat and easy-going. It starts from the branch road up to Mount Olympus.

Sample chocolates in Platres.

The Troodos mountains are an unlikely place for a chocolatier – so if only for that reason, it's worth popping in and buying Cyprus-made chocolates at the **Platres**

Chocolate Workshop (www.cypruschocolate.com). The Cyprus-themed flavours include *commandaria* (sweet wine), Cyprus coffee, *zivaneia* (firewater) and *loukoumi* (Turkish delight); the alcoholic *zivaneia*, in my uneducated opinion, was the pick of the bunch.

Paphos Forest

If you like twisting, turning mountain roads, Paphos Forest – the vast, lightly populated expanse between the high Troodos and Polis – is for you. The area is a forested wilderness, inhabited by the elusive moufflon, a wild sheep that is the symbol of Cyprus. Moufflon can only be reliably found at the conservation enclosures near the main road junction and landmark in the wilderness, Stavros tis Psokas.

Just drive.

Sometimes, it's not about where you're going, but what you do on the way – and if you visit Paphos Forest, then you'd better enjoy **driving**, because that's how you'll be spending most of your time. The roads here are a seemingly endless series of twists and turns, revealing view upon view of pine forests, hills and even sea.

Go moufflon-spotting.

No matter what route you take across Paphos Forest – and there are only a few metalled roads to choose from – you'll usually wind up at **Stavros tis Psokas** at some point, and at that point you'll be itching to stretch your legs. It's a great opportunity to take the little path that leads around the outside of a largish moufflon enclosure, and to see what a moufflon looks like at first hand. Very often, they can be quite hard to spot, even though you know they're there.

Visit Cedar Valley.

A nature reserve devoted to thousands of ancient cedars, **Cedar Valley** is a majestic sight – and all the more majestic for being in the heart of a pine forest. After mile upon mile of forest road, the sudden change in the colour and shape of the landscape takes your breath away.

If you want to plan ahead, Sherpa Walking Holidays (www.sherpa-walking-holidays.co.uk) offer a self-guided Troodos walking tour with Cedar Valley on the itinerary.

Marvel at Kykkos.

Though modern, **Kykkos Monastery** (www.kykkos-museum.cy.net) is one of the richest and best known monasteries on the island – and though in recent years it's not quite such a pilgrimage to get here as it used to be (the old earth track to the monastery has been paved) it's still a long way from anywhere at all. There's a courtyard with split-level colonnade; and lavish modern frescoes abound, inside and outside the church of the Panayia.

Kykkos was where the first president of Cyprus, Archbishop Makarios III, was admitted as a novice, and where he was buried; in 2008 a giant bronze statue of him was moved from outside the Archbishop's Palace in Nicosia – where it was considered too big for its surroundings – and brought here.

Marathasa and Solea

The Marathasa and Solea valleys, north of Mount Olympus, are home to many of the most famous "painted churches" of Troodos – Unesco-listed Orthodox churches with original frescoes ranging from the 12th to the 15th centuries. As the most identifiable landmarks, they make a great excuse to tour the villages; for an in-depth guide to these and other churches, I recommend Gwynneth der Parthog's *Byzantine and Medieval Cyprus*.

Visit Ayios Ioannis Lampadistis.

You can't miss the monastery of **Ayios Ioannis Lampadistis** (St John the Bringer of Light; www.islebright.com/links/250cy/077) in Kalopanayiotis – the monastery is on the opposite side of the Marathasa valley from the village, and visible from virtually every point. To reach it, you cross by car via a rickety-looking wooden bridge – and that worrisome experience over, there are three churches to see in the large, extensively restored complex, dating from the 11th to the 15th centuries.

Back in the village itself, the upmarket **Casale Panayiotis** (+357 22 952444, www.casalepanayiotis.com) occupies a number of agrotourism-style apartments, each marked with wooden signs – though it's still a work in progress, with more properties to be added.

Stay at the Mill in Kakopetria.

For a central, family-friendly base on the northern slopes of Troodos, near many of the most famous Unesco-listed churches, the **Mill Hotel** (+357 22 922536, www.cymillhotel.com) in Kakopetria is a pretty good bet. The hotel, a vast building on the site of a 17th-century flour mill, boasts large, alpine-style rooms, each with a balcony, from which the view extends all the way down the Solea valley to the north. On the top floor there is a large restaurant, again with family appeal, where the speciality is the fresh Troodos trout, bought locally and from Phoini village. The village square is full of cafes and tavernas – attractive by day, but with perhaps too much neon at night.

As for the churches, **Ayios Nikolaos tis Stegis** (St Nicholas of the Roof; www.islebright.com/links/250cy/080) is probably the most famous painted church of Troodos, and only just to the south-west of Kakopetria; Galata, just to the north, is home to the church of **Panayia Podythou** (www.islebright.com/links/250cy/081), in a field just outside the village.

See the church of Asinou, Nikitari.

Not a huge distance off the main Nicosia-Troodos road, but still off the beaten tourist track, the little church of **Asinou** (www.islebright.com/links/250cy/082) occupies a peaceful position in a valley flanked by forests of pine. It's pretty enough on the outside – a rectangular stone church with a typical Troodos-style wooden pitched roof, it's bound by a little stone-wall courtyard and even has a separate belltower – but the real treasures are inside, where you can find a huge number of colourful frescoes from the 12th to the 17th centuries, including a depiction of the "40 Martyrs of Sebaste" huddled together on a frozen lake, and graphic panels showing tortures meted out after the Last Judgment. To see inside the church, make sure you ask first at the coffee shop in Nikitari, a few miles north; if it does happen to be locked, you'll need room in your car for the custodian to squeeze in with you.

Find traces of the Cyprus railway.

Cyprus has no railway, right? Wrong. In fact a railway ran along the plain from Famagusta in the east as far as Nicosia, then on to Morphou and finally extended up to Evryhou, here in the Solea valley. The **old station in Evryhou** has long been promised to be a railway museum, but although nothing has come to fruition yet, it's possible (though you may need a 4x4) to find the little station building with its red British-style postbox – unusual, because after independence, the postboxes in Cyprus were all painted yellow.

Look in at the Two Flowers, Pedoulas.

It's hardly the height of luxury, but that's not the point: the **Two Flowers** (+357 22 952372, www.twoflowershotel.com) is an old-school restaurant and hotel that does a good-value Cypriot meal, with an unbeatable view of the valley below. It was here, incidentally, that I had my first taste of Filfar, a Cypriot brand of orange liqueur.

Pitsilia

Pitsilia is a large, fairly ill-defined region stretching east from central Troodos – taking in agricultural centres such as

Agros and Kyperounda, but also some Unesco-listed churches, fine wineries and commanding views.

Taste wine at the Tsiakkas winery, Pelendri.

On the road from Platres to Pelendri is the **Tsiakkas winery**, one of the most interesting on the island – and where a modern tasting room overlooks a steep, terraced vineyard on a protected, northerly slope. Here, you can taste Cypriot wine, take a winery tour – and buy wine to take home in a "wine skin" that, in the event of a breakage, will stop the wine leaking all over the clothes in your suitcase.

Among the products you can taste here are an unfortified style of *commandaria*, which isn't sold commercially but is paler and more refined than the traditional sweet *commandaria* of Cyprus; a "red *zivaneia*" that gets its colour from *commandaria* barrels; and a *xynisteri* (white) and a *vamvakada* (red), both Cypriot native varieties. Tsiakkas is also experimenting with lesser-known varieties such as *yiannoudi*.

Visit the Unesco-listed church at Pelendri.

You can easily combine a trip to the Tsiakkas winery with a visit to the 12th-century church of **Timios Stavros** (www.islebright.com/links/250cy/084). The church has an amazing array of Byzantine frescoes – most notably, the fresco of the pregnant Mary meeting Elizabeth, mother of John the Baptist, in which both women are depicted with their unborn children inside them. It's in a striking location, too, overlooking a valley on a little promontory just downhill of the main road through the village; it's possible to drive down, so just follow the brown signs. If the church is locked, ask for the keyholder at the last but one house on the right (the one with the vines and the blue road name on the wall).

Buy traditional products in Agros...

Agros is one of the largest villages in these parts – and a good place to stop and buy traditional Cyprus produce. Try the local smokery, **Kafkalia** (+357 25 521426), which smokes its own products including *tsamarella*, goat rump liberally seasoned with oregano and salt – much nicer than it sounds – then, down the hill, find **Ta Spitakia tis Nikis** (+357 25 521400, www.nikisweets.com.cy), a shop that specialises in traditional Cypriot “spoon sweets”. Tomato, watermelon, aubergine, carrot, pumpkin and kumquat are just some of the exotic ingredients, but my favourite was the *vyssino*, or sour cherry.

If you’ve ever tried the Cyprus dessert *mahalepi*, then you’ll know that rosewater is a big thing in Cyprus – and Agros, being a centre of Cypriot rose cultivation, organises an annual **Rose Festival** in May to celebrate the fact. Practically anywhere in the village, you can buy traditional rose products – perhaps unsurprisingly given the Cypriot sweet tooth, these include rose petal jam.

... and consider staying at the Rodon.

If you start to feel at home in Agros, you could stay at the **Rodon Hotel** (+357 25 521201, www.rodonhotel.com) on the edge of the village. It’s a large, three-star establishment, set up for group excursions into the hills; it has an unpretentious air, tennis courts, and views of the valley from its terrace.

Get away from it all at Askas.

If you've a romantic bone in your body, you'll love the tiny little village of **Askas**, with its warren of steep, cobbled streets, half-dilapidated buildings and general air of being in the back of beyond. About 10 years ago I stayed in an agrotourism studio at **Evghenia's House** here (via www.agrotourism.com.cy), which offered good-value accommodation with great views over the valley and the red rooftops of the village; it seems to be still there, and to reach it you take the track downhill opposite the coffee shop. There's also a short, circular nature trail, which climbs clockwise among the hazel and walnut trees in the hills above the village.

Drive from Fterikoudi to Alona.

There are many pretty roads in Cyprus – but the **road from Fterikoudi to Alona** is an absolute belter. Clinging to the north side of the mountain, it winds among vines and almond trees with views of majestic crags and the north-facing valley below. Just be careful of what's coming the other way – it's single track – and if you want to see it in its current state, get here before the ever-prolific Road-Widening Department does.

Walk from one Unesco-listed church to another.

The 13th-century church of **Panayia tou Araka** or **Panayia tou Arakos** (www.islebright.com/links/250cy/088), between the villages of Lagoudera and Saranti, is one of my favourites in the Troodos – not least because its unassuming, timber exterior belies the riot of frescoes within. Inside, there is a step where the Rigaina or semi-mythical "Queen" of Cyprus was thought to have "wished", according to George Jeffery's early 20th-century account[6]. The church sits by a shaded cliff edge where you can admire the Troodos views in the heat of the day – and has an 800-year-old olive tree in its grounds, propped up by a metal bar to stop it falling in the road.

Stavros tou Ayiasmati (www.islebright.com/links/250cy/089), meanwhile, with its 15th-century frescoes by Philip Goul, is some distance away by road, nestling in an idyllic, forested flank of a hill; it's a long way from the nearest village and often locked, so to ensure access, ask for the custodian at the coffee shop in Platanistasa village on your way through.

Perhaps the most interesting way to visit both churches – even if you end up finding one locked – is via a linear **nature trail** (www.islebright.com/links/250cy/090) leading between the two. It's a fairly challenging, 7km walk that leads over the ridge skirting the Kourtellorotsos peak, via almond trees and forests of pine – but if you like to combine activity with a bit of culture, it's a particularly fun day out.

Machairas Forest

The area around the monastery of Machairas, in the eastern Troodos, is known as Machairas Forest – not that that greatly distinguishes it from the rest of Troodos, which is also forested. It's an area of scenic trails, cobblestone villages and vertiginous cliffs.

Have lunch at Fikardou.

If you're driving around the northern slopes of Troodos, the restored village of **Fikardou** makes a great target for lunch. The **Yiannakos taverna** here (+357 22 633311), sheltered by a forested ridge and looking out over the terracotta rooftops clustered against a hill, serves a fantastic mountain *meze* – including pickled vegetables, sheep's yoghurt from Avdimou served unpretentiously in a plastic pot, tender *afelia* (marinated pork) and some of the best *loukanika* (spicy Cyprus sausages) I've had. Portion sizes are large even by Cyprus standards, judging by the immense *kleftiko* (slow-cooked lamb) at the next table, at any rate. Village wine is served in a gourd, and after lunch you can wander up to the little **rural museum** (+357 22 634731, www.islebright.com/links/250cy/091) in the village; you'll be in need of a stroll.

Stop at the monastery of Machairas.

The huge, attractively sited **Machairas monastery** (+357 22 359334, www.islebright.com/links/250cy/092), from which the area takes its name, was founded in the 12th century; but it became famous in the 20th as the hiding place of Grigoris Afxentiou, one of the leaders of the violent EOKA campaign against British rule, who took refuge here, disguising himself as a monk. Just below the monastery is the hideout where, after British troops caught up with him in 1957,

Afxentiou fought to his death; the little cave lies at the foot of a cliff path opposite a sheer drop, and has been turned into a shrine adorned with wreaths in Greek blue and white.

The monastery itself is imposing but relatively modern; in spring, swifts can be seen diving among the arches of the colonnade, while a flying buttress with a walkway on top is one of its more interesting architectural features.

Walk the forest trails.

Machairas Forest is criss-crossed with an increasing number of nature trails – many of which converge at the **Kionia picnic site**, on the ridge near Machairas peak, an area which commands views not only north to the Mesaoria plain, but south to the sea. From Kionia you can walk east to Profitis Ilias (www.islebright.com/links/250cy/093) or north-east to Mantra tou Kampiou (another picnic site; www.islebright.com/links/250cy/094); it's possible to link these two trails to make a 15km circle, via earth roads, though this would require a printout of a satellite map.

Just before the Afxentiou hideout near Machairas monastery, meanwhile, is the start of the relatively new **Machairas-Politiko trail** (leaflets available locally) that leads 5.5km north down the Pediaios river valley – best walked downhill, you would imagine, but be aware when arranging transport that the trail does not go all the way to Politiko village, but to a point on the road 7km short of it.

Wander the cobblestone streets of Lazanias.

Lazanias is the kind of village you like to stop in for a half-hour or so to break up a long drive. Its cobblestone streets are great for a little potter, and the balconies and doorways are decorated with hibiscus, vines and hanging gourds. There's a restaurant here, the Estiatorio Mageia Lazania, which serves *kleftiko* and *souvla* on a weekend – and there's a Troodos-style church with stone belltower, opposite which is one of the many British water fountains you see in Cyprus, this one marked "ER 1957".

4. Things to do in Larnaca & Ayia Napa

Once the island's main commercial centre, Larnaca (official spelling: Larnaka) was the first sight of Cyprus for many a 19th-century traveller – and since 1974, when the airport moved here, it has been the first sight for most modern visitors. It's a friendly, fast-changing town with great beaches and a surprisingly arty vibe.

Also in the Larnaca region are villages such as touristy Lefkara, the old lace-producing centre; the fishing harbour of Zygi; and the villages near Kalavasos that increasingly specialise in rural tourism, and benefit from being roughly equidistant from Larnaca, Nicosia and Limassol.

East of Larnaca is the Sovereign Base Area of Dhekelia, which is British soil[5]; beyond that is the region around Ayia Napa – technically in the Famagusta region, but included here, because since 1974 it's been cut off from Famagusta by the Green Line. Ayia Napa is of course known as a beach and party capital, but it also boasts some culture of its own, and is striking distance from Cape Greco, a small national park in the far south-east corner of the island.

In the city: Larnaca

Good beaches, some excellent shopping, a wide array of sights, and some decent bars and tavernas, all within a fairly well-defined central zone, make Larnaca one of the most accessible cities in Cyprus, and the only one that really cuts it as a city-break destination – especially thanks to the increasing number of good city-centre hotels.

Stay in a city-centre hotel.

Last time I visited Larnaca, I stayed in the **Achilleos City Hotel** (+357 24 624150, www.achilleoshotel.com) – and I wasn't disappointed. The hotel boasts tastefully renovated rooms, is right in the city centre, has extremely friendly staff and serves a good top-floor breakfast; despite its central location, it's also well soundproofed from any outdoor noise. It's perhaps not on the most salubrious street (the back of a McDonald's is nearby), but that was the only real downside, and I'd recommend it.

Gaze up at the church of St Lazarus.

You can't miss Larnaca's most famous Christian monument: the 10th-century **St Lazarus church** (+357 24 652498, www.islebright.com/links/250cy/096) in the centre of the town. In many ways the church is an architectural oddity, with a Latinate, 19th-century campanile sitting astride an essentially Byzantine structure; but the overall effect seems to work. Inside, meanwhile, there is a magnificent gold iconostasis – to the right of which is the entrance to a small crypt, where lies the supposed tomb of Lazarus. An icon museum occupies a colonnaded wing on the church's seaward side.

Even if you're not interested in churches, it's worth coming to the area around the church – which has been tastefully pedestrianised in recent years, helping give central Larnaca a far more upmarket focus than the bars and restaurants of Phinikoudes beach.

Relax at the Art Cafe 1900.

The interior of the belle epoque **Art Cafe 1900** (+357 24 653027, www.artcafe1900.com.cy), situated just off Zenonos Kitieos (Zenon of Kition Street), evokes turn-of-the-century Paris rather than Cyprus – aptly, perhaps, given Larnaca's long history as a trading port. The building is split into two areas: the restaurant on the top floor has high ceilings with walls covered with art; while the bar on the ground floor is a more modern bohemia, with arty film posters, and 85 types of beer from Waggle Dance to Delirium Tremens, which can't be bad.

Walk the salt lake to the Kamares aqueduct...

To see the wilder side of Larnaca, head to the **salt lake** on the west of the city – which is usually dry in summer but fills up over the winter season, when the flamingos arrive, after which the lake takes on a hazy turquoise hue.

From the point where the Artemidos road meets the salt

lake, a flat nature trail leads along its edge to the main surviving section of the **Kamares aqueduct** – a grandiose series of arches, which once brought water several miles to Larnaca from the Tremithos river to the west of the city, but now parallel to a main road. The aqueduct is Ottoman, built in the 18th century, but it is thought there was a Roman aqueduct on the same route prior to that.

... and go hunting for the rest of it.

What's lesser known is that, following the line of the Kamares aqueduct "upstream" to the south-west, it's possible to find other **surviving sections** of the old structure. A second series of arches lies in fields about 1-2km south-west of the first, near the Larnaca Karting Centre; and there is a long, lower third section in fields between the E316 and the A3 highway, north of Dromolaxia. Both sections are visible on satellite maps, which you'll probably need to print out and bring with you; I haven't ventured out to find them yet, so let me know how you get on.

Visit Gallery Kypriaki Gonia.

A semi-restored old house, with tiled floor and slightly bohemian air, is home to the established **Kypriaki Gonia** (+357 24 621109, www.gallerykypriakigonia.com.cy; translation: "Cypriot corner"), a gallery which shows mainly paintings by Greek and Cypriot artists – in a range of contemporary and traditional styles.

The engaging owner, Nikos Psatharis, also organises **auctions** (www.psatharis-auctions.com.cy) which are held at the Nicosia Hilton.

Have dinner at Taverneio.

The full name of this restaurant, opposite the currently closed Art and Clay potters' collective, is **Taverna Stou Rousia** (+357 99 243870, Nikolaou Laniti 26); but the sign simply says "Taverneio" in Greek script. Whatever you call it, it's a fantastic place for a light evening meal, especially if (as is usual in Cyprus) you happen to have had an extensive lunch. The menu includes home-made dips – always a good sign – exceptional *halloumi*, and a proper *souvlaki* in pitta for not much more than you'd pay at a takeaway. The atmosphere, too, is first-rate: in winter, you sit in an old, stone converted building; in summer, you eat outside in the alley, with tables laid neatly with blue-check tablecloths.

Visit the Hala Sultan Tekke mosque.

On the other side of the salt lake from the city is the **Hala Sultan Tekke** (www.islebright.com/links/250cy/100) – an Islamic shrine which you shouldn't miss, even if you're only passing through Larnaca with an hour or two to go before you have to be at the airport. The site is a shrine to Umm Haram (Hala Sultan), nurse of the prophet Mohammed. According to tradition, she fell from a mule during a Genoese counter-raid, broke her neck, and was buried on the spot. The resulting mosque occupies a romantic position among palm trees on the edge of the salt lake – and feels like a place that time forgot.

Wander around Scala.

Every Friday at 10am, the Cyprus Tourism Organisation (CTO) organises a tour of the place the Greek Cypriots call

Scala (literally "ladder") – the old Turkish Cypriot area of the city. It's worth going on the tour to see the old Ottoman architecture, wander under the barrel vault of the Buyuk Tzami (mosque), visit the ceramic workshops mainly around Ak Deniz (see below) and then to walk back along the narrow seafront at Piyale Pasha. Along the way is the small **Larnaca Fort** (+357 24 322710, www.islebright.com/links/250cy/101), where you can wander up on the ramparts for a sea view and better look at the Buyuk Tzami's minaret; there's also an old "gallows room", last used by the British for hanging prisoners in 1945.

A walking tour of the city centre, Larnaca Past and Present, takes place at 10am on Wednesdays.

Buy original Cypriot pottery.

The street of Ak Deniz, at the far end of the Scala walking tour (see previous entry), is known for its pottery workshops, which are well worth visiting.

The first, on your left as you head away from the sea, is the workshop of **Efthymios Symeou** (+357 24 650338, www.studioceramicscyprus.com), a former engineer. Symeou works in a range of styles, including stoneware and ceramics with fish motifs, but his most interesting work is his reinterpretation of Byzantine Cypriot *sgraffito* pottery, echoing its naive figures and green-yellow colour palette. Symeou also offers pottery courses.

A few doors down is the workshop of the potter **Stavros Stavrou** (+357 24 624491, www.stavrosceramics.com), who also has a prominent shop in town, the **Flamma Arts Gallery** (+357 24 625530; Zenonos Kitieos 113) – if one is closed, he will often be at the other. The gallery includes some modern and fun ceramics with motifs of fish and birds, jewellery, and even teapots; there is also an eminently giftable ceramic plaque which reads *kalosorisate* – "welcome" – in Greek script.

Let your kids spot planes at Mackenzie Beach.

Mackenzie Beach, south of Larnaca, isn't exactly the most secret beach in Cyprus – but nor is it somewhere you should dismiss, as it has two fantastic attractions for children. First, you can walk a very long way before getting out of your depth; and second, all the flights at Larnaca Airport land directly over the beach, with the runway starting less than 200m from the shoreline – so your kids can watch the planes up close, and even see them come right up close to the beach before turning round and taking off. For any aeroplane-obsessed little one, this makes it something of a dream come true – especially as it allows some extra beach time on the first or last day of a holiday.

In June, celebrate the festival of the flood.

An Orthodox festival with pagan roots, **Kataklysmos** is the "festival of the flood" – celebrated with gusto in towns by the sea, and in Larnaca in particular. The Larnaca festival begins with fireworks and includes concerts, dances, poetry performances, shadow puppet plays, sporting contests from kayak races to beach volleyball, and even – as part of the 2012 programme, anyway – a "folk singing and shepherd flute contest". All in all it's a fun time to be in Larnaca, and well worth visiting for.

Try to figure out the Pierides Museum.

If you're fond of puzzles, I'd recommend the **Pierides Museum** (+357 24 814555, www.islebright.com/links/250cy/105). At the time of my visit, this extensive private collection was juxtaposed with the work of a modern artist, Dimitris Alithinos, with signed copies by the artist even interspersed in the archaeological displays – leaving the visitor struggling to work out where the art ends and the history begins, which is of course what the artist intended. There was even a play on the artist's name, as the Greek word *alithinos* means "genuine".

Postmodern interpretations aside, there are some pretty pieces here including some Cypro-geometric jugs and a potentially fascinating cartographic collection.

Dive to the wreck of the Zenobia.

The **Zenobia** (www.islebright.com/links/250cy/106), which sank just off Larnaca on its maiden voyage in 1980, is one of the most impressive sunken wrecks in the Mediterranean, and the reason many divers come to Cyprus. On a guided dive for suitably qualified divers, it's possible to see the cargo of 104 articulated lorries that sank with the vessel – including one loaded with eggs that are at least partly intact.

Walk past the Touzla mosque.

Hidden away in the back streets of Larnaca is the architecturally interesting **Touzla mosque** – once the 12th or 13th-century Catholic church of the Holy Cross, it was converted to a mosque after the Ottoman invasion; and was once even Byzantine. The mosque may be closed, but it's notable for its massive supporting buttresses, its arched colonnade, its restored minaret and even the dark green wood used in its restoration. You'll find it just west of Plateia Mitropoleos.

The mosque can be added to a visit to the best of the ruins of **Ancient Kition** (+357 24 304115, www.islebright.com/links/250cy/107) – one of the original Cypriot city-states, home to a major Phoenician civilisation. Much of Kition lies buried under the modern city, but in "Area II", amid the suburbs, are the remains of a shrine to the Phoenician fertility goddess, Astarte.

Look in at the municipal gallery.

The renovated old customs warehouses in Europe Square, central Larnaca, are very easy on the eye. Part of the space has been converted into a diverting **municipal art gallery** (+357 24 658848) with some interesting pieces: not least a "Kalikantzaroi" print by Cypriot printmaker Hambis Tsangaris, showing the mischievous goblins of Greek tradition; and a challenging tower sculpture by Athena Antoniadou which begs interpretation.

In the same building, the interesting-sounding **Historic Archives Museum** had closed for renovation on my visit. If you're researching an aspect of Larnaca history, however, this is the place to come, as the archives office is on the floor above.

On the coast: east to Ayia Napa and Cape Greco

You don't tend to visit to Ayia Napa if you're looking for the "traditional" Cyprus; it mainly caters for the hotel-beach-club crowd, and it does so very well. But that's not to say that the area lacks beauty. Down in the far south-east corner of Cyprus is the Cape Greco National Park – while many of the popular beaches would be utterly idyllic if it weren't for the crowds.

Visit Ayia Napa Monastery.

The Greek Orthodox **Ayia Napa Monastery** (+357 23 721284, www.islebright.com/links/250cy/108) is an island of austerity amid the nightlife of Ayia Napa – but it was here first, and it will probably outlast it too. Inside, a 16th-century church is cut into the rock, while the palm trees and arched colonnades give the place an exotic, eastern appeal.

Discover Kyrenia II.

There's much to recommend about the **Thalassa Museum of the Sea** (+357 23 816366, www.islebright.com/links/250cy/109) in Ayia Napa – but the standout exhibit is *Kyrenia II*, a functional replica of the famous ancient ship which sank off Kyrenia in around 300 BC (the original was salvaged in the 1960s and remains to this day in Kyrenia Castle; see page 108). Manned by a crew of four, the replica achieved 2,000 miles of sailing before being exhibited here.

Among other highlights, there's a reconstructed

papyrella, a boat made from reeds, made to try to explain how obsidian[7] could have been transported around the Cyclades islands 11,000 years ago; a pretty geometric *askos* (vessel) in the shape of a fish; a bizarre selection of stuffed sea life, including dolphins and turtles; the skeleton of the long-extinct Cypriot pygmy hippo; and scale models of both a pygmy hippo and a pygmy elephant.

Have lunch at Liopetri Potamiou.

Potamos (+357 99 637301, www.potamosrestaurant.com) at Liopetri Potamiou is in a great spot for lunch, right on the shore of an inlet dotted with little fishing boats; if it weren't for the Mediterranean cuisine, you could almost imagine you were by a cove in Brittany. There's a good atmosphere at weekends, and in my opinion the thing to order is the cuttlefish, squid or octopus, all of which on my visit were fresh, not previously frozen; I can speak for the cuttlefish (*soupies*), which were excellent. The huge "island salad", meanwhile, is a departure from the norm, and well defended with pickled caper thorns. The courtyard tree, festooned with gourds, adds to the hospitable feel.

Chill out at Ayia Thekla.

Most of the beaches west of Ayia Napa are busy even out of season – but if you prefer things a little quieter, head down to **Ayia Thekla**. This is a sheltered, sandy beach with palm trees and a decent snack bar, though looks a bit rocky underwater, so bring goggles or a snorkel. The name comes from the simple, concrete church at one end of the bay, its roof painted an appealing blue.

The closer you get to Ayia Napa, of course, the busier the beaches get: **Makronissos**, featuring a little headland boasting some ancient tombs, has a bar with music on the beach; well-known **Nissi Beach**, a bay with a sandy causeway that leads to a little forested peninsula, is a full-blown resort with waiting taxis, shops and good hotels close by – so it's very busy, even in spring.

Visit Konnos Bay – out of season.

Konnos Bay on the east coast is another picture-postcard spot: a sandy beach at the centre of a semicircle of cliffs forested with pines, with a shady cafe-kiosk providing great sea views and welcome respite from the sun. The trouble is that everyone knows this, so, unless you're cool with crowds, it's somewhere you may wish to save for the off-season. The cafe-kiosk, by the way, is run by the nearby Grecian Park Hotel.

Walk around Cape Greco.

Cape Greco, the national park occupying the south-east extremity of the island, is an oasis of beauty between the developments of Ayia Napa and Protaras. Sadly, the far end of the cape isn't open to tourists, because it's used as a military base – but the network of **Cape Greco nature trails** more than makes up for this.

Sticking to the coast almost all the way, for example, you could walk the 4km from Ayioi Anargyroi – an east-facing headland with its eponymous chapel, still used for weddings and christenings – all the way round to the Sea Caves on the opposite coast, a photogenic spot where the sea has sculpted the rock into a series of arches and caves (www.islebright.com/links/250cy/111; there's also a rubbish dump nearby, but try to ignore that).

Heading in the opposite direction, you could also walk from Ayioi Anargyroi to Konnos Bay via a shorter trail (www.islebright.com/links/250cy/112). This would make quite a fun day out: parking at Ayioi Anargyroi, walking for half an hour along the coast, chilling out at the beach and cafe, then retracing your weary steps at the end of the day.

Drive along the Dhekelia old road.

Although it's a fairly unattractive stretch of coastline, with a power station and not the best beaches, it's interesting to drive down the **old road** which runs past the British garrison in the Sovereign Base Area of Dhekelia (eastern SBA)[5]. On "Cessac beach" here, **Lambros Fish and Chips** (+357 24 723206) – on a covered terrace built over the sea – does a roaring trade on a Saturday night.

Visit the buffer zone village of Pyla.

The word *pyla* means "gate" in Greek – and the village of **Pyla** (Turkish: Pile) gets that name, no doubt, because it is enclosed by cliffs, to create a natural geological gateway toward higher ground to the north. But these days it's a cultural and political gateway, too – Pyla is a mixed Greek Cypriot and Turkish Cypriot village that's entirely within the UN buffer zone which runs along the Green Line. It's one of the few places in Cyprus where it's possible to buy a bottle of Keo in one shop and a bottle of Efes in another – and well worth a visit for that. Heading north from Pyla, you head briefly into the eastern SBA[5] before reaching the Pergamos crossing on the Green Line.

For more on life in Pyla, read *Echoes from the Dead Zone* by Yiannis Papadakis, an anthropologist who lived here for a year in 1994/95.

On the coast: west to Zygi

The coast west of Larnaca is quiet and fairly empty, with drivable roads and the odd stopping point along the way.

Just drive.

Once you're out of the suburbs, the **old road west out of Larnaca** can be a joy to drive. Die-straight, with flat expanses of yellowing fields to your right and the Mediterranean sea close by to the left, it's a place to just enjoy being behind the wheel in Cyprus.

Stop off at the church at Kiti.

There are a few churches in Cyprus that stop you in your tracks and make you want to get out of the car – and the stone church of **Panayia Angeloktisti** in Kiti (+357 24 424646, www.islebright.com/links/250cy/113), with its mix of domes and juxtaposed curved roofs, falls firmly into that category. Its exterior beauty is nothing compared to its primary treasure: a gilded, 6th-century mosaic of the Virgin Mary, standing on a stool. The mosaic is in the apse (the semicircular bit behind the icon screen where the priest stands); bizarrely, it predates the church, which was built in the 10th century. Stranger still is the church's mix of architectural styles: the area through which you enter is in fact a 13th-century Latin chapel, simply tacked on to the outside of the building.

In the courtyard, there's a pistachio tree known in English as the "Mount Atlas mastic" – *tremithos* in Greek – which, a sign informs us, is 14 metres high. More to the point, under the tree there are some cafe tables where you can enjoy a *limonada* or a *mahalepi*.

Detour to Perivolia.

Perivolia, just outside Larnaca, is a self-contained resort with a slight backwater feel but no shortage of tavernas and bars. It's a fairly decent place to base yourself if you want to be on the sea but still have a bit of peace. While here, take a look at the **Pyrgos tis Rigainas** (Tower of the Queen), a little folly on a hill.

Eat fish at Zygi.

The fishing village of **Zygi** has, of late, been a pretty unfortunate place. Scarcely a few months after the town's marina had been prettily renovated, there was a major munitions explosion at a nearby naval base – which killed 12 people, took out the main power station of the island, and blew out virtually every window in the village. The explosion – which also caused widespread power cuts – was the number one political issue on the island for the months that followed. Zygi, for its part, has simply had to clean up and do its best to attract people back.

Zygi remains an atmospheric spot, well worth visiting

for lunch – and popular with Cypriots on high days and holidays, who come to eat here in their hundreds.

Drive down the valley of Ayios Theodoros.

The valley road that leads from the highway to the coast via **Ayios Theodoros** offers some unexpected upland scenery, being so near to the sea. The road here passes through a wide, green valley, through a village centre which straddles a dry river bed (immeasurably altered, no doubt, by the damming of the river upstream); before winding past orange and citrus orchards via a narrowing gorge, rich with birdlife, before opening up to olive groves, a delta, and the sea.

Into the hills: Kalavasos and around

Between the Mari power station and Larnaca, the motorway cuts inland, bringing rapid access to inland villages such as Skarinou, Choirokitia, Kalavasos and Tochni. Although this is hardly the prettiest part of Cyprus, the villages here have made the most of their combination of traditional charm and accessible position, by promoting themselves as bases for agrotourism holidays.

Visit Kalavasos – and maybe even stay.

Friendly **Kalavasos**, set in the valley below the huge Kalavasos Dam, has just the right mix of smartness and faded charm – and if there was a competition for "Cyprus in

Bloom 2012", then this place, with its gardens of geranium, hibiscus and palms, would win it. Walking up the semi-pedestrianised main street there's a little art gallery, owned by Michalis Mozoras, who creates artefacts such as angels and statuettes from fragments of pottery and stones.

If you wanted to stay in Kalavasos, there are plenty of agrotourism properties which you can book through Cyprus Villages (www.cyprusvillages.com.cy) – and there's also the upmarket Library Hotel (+357 24 817071, www.libraryhotelcyprus.com), whose 11 rooms each boast a different style of tiling. I've not stayed the night, so can't judge the service, but the hotel seems a relaxing spot, with a pleasant, split-level courtyard overlooked by a minaret, and a library reception which is like nothing else in Cyprus.

Join the agrotourism crowd at Tochni.

As beautiful as Kalavasos, but more affected by motorway noise, **Tochni** is another village that's largely been given over to agrotourism. The village is built across a V-shaped valley, so if you visit the village centre, it's a steep walk down and a thigh-wrenching climb to get back up again. There are plenty of facilities for tourists: the Nostos taverna (+357 24 333122) in the centre of town is an atmospheric early-evening spot, and there's a nice-looking *kafeneio* for breakfasts. On my visit in 2012, the English-run Tochni Heritage (www.tochniheritage.com), in a courtyard right next to the river, was just starting out; it offered light lunches and had plans to open a taverna and apartments.

As for accommodation, many properties can be booked through Cyprus Villages (see previous entry) – but also consider Eveleos Cottages, part of the Filokypros agro-tourism business (www.filokypros.com), offering comfortable little apartments with a good pool.

Climb the hill to Choirokitia.

With all the ancient Greek shrines and Roman mosaics in Cyprus, it's easy to pass over the island's Neolithic heritage. But **Choirokitia** (www.islebright.com/links/250cy/118), just off the Limassol-Larnaca highway, is home to the site where, 9,000 years ago, Stone Age Cypriots lived. Once you've climbed the hill, it's possible to wander around the remains of the round, single-storey dwellings here – and view some reconstructed versions too. The only problem is that the site is marred by the nearby highway – a fact that becomes all too obvious as the roar of the cars gets ever louder on the way down.

Seek out the Lady of the Field.

West of Choirokitia, down a bumpy dirt track and in the middle of some fields, is the **Panayia tou Kampou** or Lady of the Field – a squat, cruciform Byzantine church, on the probable site of a battlefield where, in 1426, King Janus of Cyprus was defeated and captured by a raiding Mameluke army; the church would have existed at the time, though it has been slightly extended since. Nearby, meanwhile, there are the remains of a Knights Templar *commanderie* or fort, itself destroyed in 1426. The view of the two sites is best from the benches by a bend in the road west of the village – or rather, it would be, but for the fact that it's a busy road and there's nowhere to park safely or cross the road!

Pitch up at Tenta.
Visible from the motorway as you whizz by, the little archaeological site of **Kalavasos Tenta** (www.islebright.com/links/250cy/119) is a tiny Neolithic village showing remnants – in the form of the outlines of circular, mudbrick houses – of a civilisation that lived by the banks of the river here at the end of the 7th millennium BC. Its name, apparently, derives from a much later tradition, in which the mother of Constantine the Great is supposed to have stayed overnight here in (inevitably) a tent.

The modern, tent-style covering over Tenta is both practical and striking – it alludes to the local tradition, draws attention to the site and provides valuable protection from summer sun and winter rain. More to the point, if you're getting bored of motorway driving between Limassol and Larnaca or Nicosia, a stop here serves to break up the journey nicely.

Into the hills: Lefkara and around

Lefkara was traditionally the lace-making centre of Cyprus – and with the coming of British rule, its lace experienced a boom, with local tradespeople growing rich and building impressive mansions on the results of their labours. Modern-day Lefkara lace is a tourist-centred industry – but it's interesting to see the early 20th-century grandeur of Lefkara and nearby Kato Drys.

Take the long road via Kato Drys.

The main road from the motorway to Lefkara is a fast, if steep, highway built to handle tourist coaches – but it's worth taking the windier, prettier and more circuitous route, via the villages of Vavla and Kato Drys.

Vavla is a tiny, pretty collection of traditional stone houses clinging to a side of a hill, with commanding valley views to the east; further along the road there's also the stone convent of Ayios Minas, where you can buy both herbs and honey.

But the real attraction here is **Kato Drys**, which boasts around 30 neoclassical houses, built in the early 20th century from the profits of the lace trade. At one of the two rural museums here, attached to the **Garden Kamara Complex** (+357 24 342351), Elli Kornioti displays a collection of letters, memories associated with her grandfather, a lace trader who travelled with his work; there's also a small beekeeping museum attached.

Also, if you can, try to taste the preserves made by Elli Paraskeva at **Jar** (+357 96 476265), run out of a 1930s coffee shop – but don't make the mistake I did and find it closed: call ahead if you can, as Elli is often elsewhere, selling her produce around the island.

If you're looking for a lunch or coffee stop, Kato Drys also has a friendly *kafeneio* and a taverna.

In Lefkara, find the Castle of the Queen.

Touristy as it may be, Lefkara does have an unusual secret that isn't peddled as overtly as its lace. It comes in the form of a strange rock, known as the **Kastro tis Rigainas** or

Castle of the Queen. Jutting out of a hill east of Lefkara like a plate on the back of a stegosaurus, the rock towers over a huge plain, itself encircled by the Lefkara hills to the west and Kornos mountains to the east. Lefkarites associate it with Rigaina, the semi-mythical "Queen" of Cyprus who, it is said, brought water to the area from the Dipotamos valley.

To reach the rock, head down the zigzag dirt track that heads past the Lefkara football stadium, on a path that takes you past an idyllically situated chapel – or view it from a distance as you look east from the Lefkara-Kornos road.

By the car park in Kato Lefkara, don't miss the church.

What would tourism in Cyprus be without another stone church to look at? And the thing about this one – the 12th-century church of the **Archangel Michael** – is that it's right next to the main car park in Kato Lefkara, but easily missed. It's peaceful inside, with frescoes in arched recesses – though the area above the south door, showing part of the Archangel and an image of the Mandylion, a Byzantine relic often compared to the Turin shroud – is perhaps most interesting.

5. Things to do in Nicosia

The old walled city of Nicosia (Greek: Lefkosia) is a political oddity – the last divided capital in Europe, it's split almost exactly in two by the Green Line, which divides the government-controlled south of the island from the Turkish Cypriot administered area in the north.

This chapter covers all the government-controlled parts of the Nicosia region (Troodos and Kato Pyrgos excepted) – including the old city south of the Green Line, and often-neglected sights such as the ancient city-states of Tamassos and Idalion.

Walled city of Nicosia

It's hard to escape the reality of division in Nicosia. On streets nearest the Green Line, you'll find scruffy houses in dire need of restoration, streets suddenly ending amid oil barrels and barbed wire – and a general sense of impermanence and uncertainty, above all else.

The exception is the most important development in

Nicosia of recent years – the Ledra Street crossing, a pedestrian-only crossing-point on the Green Line, relinking the main shopping street of the town. The crossing – designed as a confidence-building initiative between Greek and Turkish Cypriots – has also made it far easier for tourists to see the grand old walled city of Nicosia, with its eight bastions and centuries of turbulent history, as a combined whole.

The entries in this section – with the exception of Open Studios Nicosia, a bicommunal initiative – cover only the south (government-controlled) part of Nicosia. For the north (Turkish Cypriot administered) part, see Chapter 6.

Take a tour.

One of the best ways of seeing old Nicosia is to take a **walking tour** of the city. Free tours start at 10am on Thursdays from the Cyprus Tourist Information Office in Laiki Yeitonia (the pedestrianised, touristy quarter); but if you can't make it at these times, you can follow the route by looking for the metal plaques, marked with the logo of the octagonal city walls, which you'll find on the ground.

There are also two tours: on Monday at 10am, a tour goes to the Kaimakli suburb, surrounded on three sides by the Green Line; while on Friday at 10am, there is a tour of Nicosia outside the walls.

Don't miss the Leventis City Museum.

The free **Leventis City Museum** (+357 22 661475, www.leventismuseum.org.cy), documenting the fascinating history of Nicosia, is a must-see. Among the exhibits, there's an introductory photo gallery grounding Cyprus sites in their chronological context; a selection of coins of medieval kings, including Peter I, who was assassinated in his own bed in 1369; a "map room" showing maps of Nicosia from the 15th to 17th centuries; a gallery devoted to representations of the last queen of Cyprus, the Venetian Caterina Cornaro, who was ousted and sent into exile; and a "Traveller's Room" showing books by 18th and 19th-century travellers to the island, open at fascinating passages that I won't spoil by giving away. Closed on my visit was a "British Gallery" covering the years of colonial rule. There's also that absolute essential, a pretty good shop.

Browse for a gift at Diachroniki.

If you're interested in reproductions of antique Cypriot maps, prints and scenes, **Gallery Diachroniki** (+357 22 680145, www.diachroniki.com) is a good place to browse for a gift. There are two branches: one in the Laiki Yeitonia, and one in Arsinois Street, just off Ledra Street. The Arsinois branch also has a huge range of original art by Cyprus-based artists.

Look in at the postal museum.

All over the old town there are signs pointing you to the **Cyprus Postal Museum** (+357 22 304711, www.islebright.com/links/250cy/122) – but it's not until you get there that you realise how interesting it is. The oldest stamps, of course, refer to the period of British colonial rule: the very oldest are just British stamps overprinted with the word "Cyprus"; later stamps, featuring Cypriot scenes, feature small denominations of Cypriot currency, "paras" and "piastres" (there were 40 paras to a piastre, and nine piastres to a British shilling); while one politically interesting stamp, no doubt dating from the early days of the Cyprus Republic, is overprinted with the words "Cypriot democracy" in Greek and Turkish – but still carries an inset picture of Queen Elizabeth II. This last stamp is also denominated in "mils" at a time when there were 1,000 mils to the Cyprus pound. Geek heaven.

Have coffee at the Weaving Mill.

Nicosia's old town has long had a bit of a cultural-intellectual vibe, and if that's your scene, the **Weaving Mill** (+357 22 762275, www.ifantourgio.org.cy) is a good place for a coffee or a drink. Describing itself as a "cultural cafe", it's a vast room with huge supporting pillars, black and white tiled floors, books across one entire wall, a stopped antique clock, a vintage pool table, bluesy music, leather sofas, and tables with chessboards neatly laid out ready for a game. There's also a huge space on the wall for projections.

Visit the galleries of Open Studios Nicosia.

The bicommunal art initiative **Open Studios Nicosia** (www.islebright.com/links/250cy/124) takes place most years in late October. For the duration of the event, Nicosia artists on both sides of the Green Line open their studios to visitors. In the past, Turkish Cypriot exhibitors have included Ayhatun Atesin, whose "ceramic shoes" formed part of her famed Silent Walk exhibition; Greek Cypriot work has included the large-scale portraiture of painter Lia

Boyiatzi. During the exhibition, you can pick up a map from the Ledra Museum, just on the south side of the Ledra Street crossing.

See the Kanakaria mosaics.

Most people know about the **Kanakaria mosaics** because of their recent history – stolen from the church of Panayia Kanakaria (page 114) in Karpas after the 1974 invasion, they were later returned to the Church of Cyprus after a US court case – but when you see them up close and personal in the **Byzantine Art Museum** (+357 22 430008, www.islebright.com/links/250cy/125), it's clear their status as a cultural treasure is more than justified. The fragments have real personality and drama, showing the young Christ, four apostles – in particular a serious St Matthew with an honest, searching expression – and a quizzical Archangel.

Have a brew at the Brew Lounge.

Despite its location right next to the tourist office, the **Brew Lounge and Tea Bar** (+357 22 100133, www.facebook.com/pages/Brew-Lounge-Tea-Bar/264347120602) is a smart, laid-back place, with a light and airy decor including ceiling fans and contemporary prints. It opens in the early evening as a tea bar, selling iced teas, traditional lemonades and iced organic filter coffee; but it also doubles up as a cocktail bar, especially so as the evening wears on, no doubt.

Buy wine at Kava To Dionysion.

If you're looking for a wine shop in the old town, **Kava To Dionysion** (+357 22 349395; Korai 33) is an interesting place to browse. It focuses mostly on international wines – but still emphasises quality, and has some good Greek and Cypriot brands including Sigalas from Santorini in Greece, Tsiakkas from Pelendri in Troodos, and Ezousa from the Paphos district.

Just east of here is a stretch of 18th-century aqueduct, recently restored.

Nicosia: outside the walls

The bulk of modern-day Nicosia is outside the city walls – where international shops and brands mix with older haunts such as the Moufflon bookshop and the Cyprus Museum.

Visit the Cyprus Museum.

The **Cyprus Museum** (www.islebright.com/links/250cy/127), just outside the Paphos Gate, hosts a dizzyingly rich array of Cypriot archaeological finds within a faded, neoclassical building – it's a must-see, but there's so much here that the key, I think, is to visit at the end of your holiday when you've visited a few sites and know where the places are.

The many highlights include the Lady of Lempa (Lemba), a limestone figurine and fertility symbol from the 3rd millennium BC (Room 1); an amazing display of hundreds of clay figurines from Ayia Irini, found in the 7th and 6th centuries BC, including a warrior god in the form of a centaur or minotaur (Room 4); lions and sphinxes from Tamassos and a marble Aphrodite from Soli (Room 5); and, in my favourite gallery, Room 7, a fantastic collection of bronze age cylinder seals, a hoard of coins found in Paphos, not to mention some exquisite beaded jewellery and glass ornaments from Hellenistic and Roman eras. That's not even the half of it, because on my visit the museum was half-closed for renovation of the exhibits.

There's a little cafe outside which, on a hot day, will probably prove welcome.

Get lost in the Moufflon.

Nicosia's **Moufflon bookshop** (+357 22 665155, www.moufflon.com.cy) is a bookshop like bookshops used to be – a treasure trove of the brilliant, the obscure and the obsolete. There are new and second-hand books here on every subject related to Cyprus, from its modern poetry to its ancient archaeology, from its twisting roads to its tortuous politics. It's not a huge shop – but if you're remotely interested in Cyprus and its people, it's possible to get lost in here for many hours.

Buy the original chewing gum from Greece.

Mastiha is the Greek word for mastic – a resin created from the sap of bushes that grow on the island of Chios, Greece, which was chewed all over the Mediterranean for centuries. More recently, the Chios Gum Mastic Growers Association set up a joint venture to create a network of shops to promote *mastiha*-based and *mastiha*-inspired products – and the **Mastiha Shop** (+357 22 445690, www.mastihashop.com) in Nicosia is one result. Here you can buy a souvenir you'll be chewing over for weeks.

Explore the British Cemetery, Nicosia.

The **British Cemetery in Nicosia** is a peaceful oasis dotted with palms and pines, bound by stone walls, in the heart of what is now a busy suburb. Among those buried here are Ken Mackenzie, who edited the Cyprus Mail newspaper during the latter days of the 1955-59 uprising against British colonial rule; and many police officers who died during that conflict, some of whose tombstones bear moving inscriptions.

The cemetery is usually kept locked, so contact the parish office of St Paul's cathedral in Nicosia (www.st-pauls-nicosia.com) if you wish to gain access.

Around Nicosia

The region around Nicosia is, it is fair to say, not the most beautiful in Cyprus – but there are some important sights, including the ancient city-states of Tamassos and Idalion and the mountain-top Stavrovouni monastery.

See the tombs at Tamassos.

Tamassos (+357 22 622619, www.islebright.com/links/250cy/131), mentioned by Homer, was a rich and ancient Cypriot city-state, famous for its supply of copper. Although the drive here is pretty uninspiring, the site is well worth a visit, thanks to its pair of underground tombs from about the 6th century BC – first excavated in 1890, they now benefit from being restored and atmospherically lit. According to a booklet you can buy on site, *Tamassos: A Brief Guide to the*

Royal Tombs, there was in fact a third tomb, but it was destroyed after 1890 by villagers searching for building material. Among more recent excavations here were large, archaic sculptures of lions and sphinxes – they're now to be found in the Cyprus Museum, where they form a substantial display in Room 5.

Visit the monastery at Ayios Iraklideios.

Just a mile or so away from Tamassos is the 18th-century convent of **Ayios Iraklideios**. A favourite among Cypriot tourists from Nicosia, it also makes an interesting side-trip if you're visiting Tamassos anyway. Within the enclosure, there's a relaxed, friendly feel about the convent's colonnaded garden cloister, where geraniums, roses and vines all thrive; inside the church, meanwhile, there are areas of glass floor, covering mosaics from an early seventh-century basilica, both in the south aisle and near the middle of the building, and there are some 18th-century frescoes.

Curiously, it seems that Ayios Iraklideios has also started to attract Cyprus' growing band of rock climbers – thanks to the outcrops of boulders among the monastery grounds. British mountaineer Huw Gilbert blogs about it at www.huwgilbert.blogspot.co.uk.

See a replica of the Idalion Tablet.

The archaeological site at **Idalion** (+357 22 444818, www.islebright.com/links/250cy/132), one of the original Cypriot city states, is huge and difficult to get a sense of – but a recently built museum provides focus. Pride of place in the museum goes to a replica of the Idalion Tablet, an inscribed slab of bronze dated to around 470 BC, adorned with a suspension ring (to hang it up with); the original was found in 1850 and is now in the National Library of France. The tablet, in Greek language and Cypro-syllabic script, refers to an agreement by a Cypriot king and his people to pay a doctor to treat those injured during the recent war with the Phoenicians; the Phoenicians were to conquer the city within 20 years, and their archive of tax records has also been found at the site.

Visit Ayios Sozomenos and Potamia.

Abandoned since intercommunal fighting in 1964, the formerly bicommunal village of **Ayios Sozemonos**, near Potamia, reeks of eerie desolation. Amid collapsing buildings, you'll find the ruins of the medieval church of Ayios Mamas – whose stone pillars stand in bare earth, supporting grand Gothic arches that reach into empty space. It's a dramatic and lonely sight.

In nearby **Potamia**, meanwhile, there are plans to renovate the west wing of a medieval palace in the village, and turn it into an attraction for visitors. According to tradition, Caterina Cornaro, the last queen of Cyprus, used to come to her summer palace here to meet a lover – though there is no evidence, sadly, to support the tale.

Buy a "tavvas" at Archontiko Papadopoulou.

Incongruously sited among the betting shops and takeaways of Kornos village is the smart **Archontiko Papadopoulou** restaurant (+357 22 531000, www.archontikopapadopoulou.com.cy), in a traditional turn-of-the-century mansion. The restaurant serves only Cypriot wine, and the menu includes such dishes as *tavvas* lamb – the *tavvas* in question being a traditional Cyprus-style stewpot. Kornos being famous as a pottery village, you can buy a *tavvas* (that is, the pot) on the premises, as there is a pottery workshop attached to the business. The restaurant also hosts food and wine matching sessions.

Enjoy the view from Stavrovouni.

There's an awe-inspiring view all the way to the sea from **Stavrovouni monastery** (+357 22 533630, www.islebright.com/links/250cy/135) – situated up a twisting, turning, mountain road off the Limassol-Nicosia highway. The monastery is thought to be one of the oldest on the island – but visiting is not much fun for a couple or a family, as women aren't allowed in.

6. Things to do in the north

What do you call the north of Cyprus? Even its name is a matter of dispute. To Greek Cypriots, the region is simply "the occupied areas"; in other words, that part of the Republic of Cyprus that has been under occupation since the Turkish invasion of 1974. To Turks and Turkish Cypriots, on the other hand, it is the "Turkish Republic of Northern Cyprus (TRNC)" – sometimes shortened to "North Cyprus" – a self-declared state whose border is the Green Line. No country apart from Turkey recognises the "TRNC" – which is why, for example, you can't fly there directly from Britain.

This book uses the geographical terms "the north" and "the north of Nicosia" to describe the areas of Cyprus and Nicosia north of the Green Line, which have been controlled by the *de facto* Turkish Cypriot administration since 1974.

To travellers, the superficial effect of arriving in the north can be like being thrown back in time. Gone are the branches of McDonald's and Starbucks that you may have just seen in the south of Nicosia; there tend to be fewer tourists, cars on the streets are typically older, roads are often less well maintained and the coastlines are less blighted by concrete hotels – though there are exceptions to these rules, of course. Depending on where in the north you go, the Turkish army also has a visible presence, with signs warning of military installations a feature of your travels, especially if you stray from touristed zones.

Ignoring Nicosia for a moment, the north of Cyprus includes three "entire" towns – the ancient ports of Famagusta and Kyrenia, and the traditionally agricultural town of Morphou. The main geographical features are the Pentadaktylos mountain range, dotted with a string of castles, which extends to become the Karpas peninsula in the north-east; and, south of the range, some of the dustiest corners of the flat Mesaoria plain.

If you're thinking of staying in the north, be aware that many, perhaps most, hotels there are built on land owned by Greek Cypriots who were forced from their property in 1974. Some hotels, though, were originally owned by Turkish Cypriots and remain so. The Republic of Cyprus carries an old list of these online (via www.islebright.com/links/250cy/136)[2] – it's dated 2007, but potentially still useful.

For more on the history of the island and the circumstances that led to its *de facto* partition, go to the Cyprus Conflict website (www.cyprus-conflict.net) – a resource which aims to recount the history of the Cyprus conflict in a balanced way.

The Green Line

Stretching for more than 180 miles across the breadth of Cyprus, from Kokkina and Limnitis in the north-west to the ghost town of Varosha in the south-east, and cutting through Nicosia along the way, the Green Line that divides Cyprus is a daily reminder of the island's troubled history. The line, which marks the final advance of the invading Turkish forces in 1974, cuts Cyprus into two regions – one controlled by the Cyprus government (the south), the other by the *de facto* Turkish Cypriot administration in the north.

Before 2003, travelling across the line was highly restricted. Since then, however, crossing points between north and south have been opened, the most notable of which is the pedestrian Ledra Street crossing, opened in 2008, which reconnects Nicosia's main shopping street. The crossing is the biggest symbolic step forward in the ponderously slow attempts to resolve the Cyprus dispute.

The following is a summary of the practicalities of crossing the Green Line. Be aware that this is not legal advice, and is only a summary of the current, practical position:

- Crossing the Green Line in either direction is, in theory at least, straightforward if you hold an EU passport; this is because Republic of Cyprus authorities tend to wave EU passport-holders through, while the Turkish Cypriot administration admits all EU citizens on production of a valid passport.
- If you do not hold an EU passport and have entered the island in the north, you are likely to be refused permission to travel into the south, on the grounds that you have entered the island from an unrecognised port of entry (considered illegal in the Republic).
- Non-EU passport holders arriving in the south and

wishing to cross to the north should have no such problems, as the Turkish Cypriot administration considers the Green Line to be its international border; but there may be visa requirements.

- In all events, it is a good idea to ask for a white "visa slip" to be stamped, rather than your passport, when crossing northwards; given that Turkish Cypriots allow this, it seems sensible.

The north of Nicosia

Just as in the south of Nicosia, it's hard to escape the reality of division in the north of the city. The difference is that the historic centre of the old town – the area comprising the Selimiye mosque and the Buyuk Han – happen to fall under Turkish Cypriot control, so there are more historical sights to see. Generally, the atmosphere in the north of Nicosia is relaxed, friendly and laid-back – though away from the tourist sights, there is a deserted feel, with some areas, such as much of Arabahmet, falling into decay.

Pause for a moment at the Ledra Street crossing.

Assuming that you're crossing into the north of Nicosia on foot from the south, perhaps the most interesting sight of all is the **Ledra Street crossing** itself. This street, Ledra Street, was, after all, the so-called Murder Mile of 1950s Cyprus during the bitter EOKA uprising against British rule; it was barricaded in 1963 during the intercommunal fighting between Greek Cypriots and Turkish Cypriots in the city;

and it remained closed off until April 2008, when it was opened as part of confidence-building efforts between the two communities. So it's a piece of modern history – and one that should give the lie to the idea that the two communities can't live together peacefully once more.

Visit the historic centre...

Nicosia's turbulent medieval and early modern history, on the other hand, are nowhere better illustrated than in its **historic centre** – where two vast, mostly Gothic edifices, replete with vaults, arched windows and flying buttresses, stand within metres of each other. The first, the **Selimiye mosque**, was built in the 13th century as the cathedral of St Sophia and converted into a mosque after the Ottoman conquest in 1570 – it still functions as a mosque, as it has done for most of its history, and its twin minarets dominate the skyline. The second, the **Bedesten** or covered market, was the even older 12th-century church of St Nicholas, originally Greek with Gothic medieval annexes; the recently renovated building now houses performances such as classical concerts and dervish dances.

The area around the mosque houses a couple of small museums: the **Sultan Mahmud II Library** (closed on my visit), though apparently its 400 books have been moved to Kyrenia; and the **Lapidary Museum**, a small collection of gargoyles, groynes and the like.

... and eat.

There's a relaxed, tourist-friendly vibe in the historic centre – and if you're looking for something to eat, there are a couple of choices. Among the buttresses just south of the mosque is **Friends of Museums**, serving Turkish *meze* on checked tablecloths; while **Sabor** (+90 392 228 8322) in a restored building opposite the mosque serves coffee and international food to a well-heeled set.

Don't miss the Buyuk Han.

The recently restored, two-storey **Buyuk Han** or "Great Inn" is a hub of tourism in the north of Nicosia, with shops and galleries occupying the cells once used to host travellers. You can get a beer or a coffee either at the popular Seddirhan restaurant in one corner, or at the more old-school Kahvehase Kafeteria opposite – at the latter, you can also order the Cyprus dessert *mahallebi* (Greek: *mahalepi*).

A couple of interesting shops are on the top floor: these include Anilir's Art Gallery, also known as the Post Office, where you can buy old postcards of Cyprus life ancient and (relatively) modern, including images of the old Cyprus railway, Cypriot doorways, and images of the inn itself; and Munuse Ozmulla, who sells handicrafts from silk.

Finally, don't neglect the outside of the *han* on Mitat Pasha street; here there's a barber, old-school coffee shop and a herb seller.

Discover dervishes at the Mevlevi Tekke.

The Mevlevi, now popularly known as the "whirling dervishes", are a spiritual order of Sufist Islam which grew to prominence in Ottoman Empire, and whose rites included a mystical, whirling dance. This **Mevlevi Tekke** (a *tekke* was a spiritual retreat for the brotherhood), was established in Nicosia a few decades after the Ottoman conquest of Cyprus – and continued until 1954, a few decades after Ataturk outlawed Sufism in Turkey. Now a museum, the domed building gives a fascinating insight into life as a dervish – alongside quotes from the *Mesnevi*, the major work of Sufist thought, written by 13th-century poet Mevlana – alongside some lifesize puppets. The *tekke* also houses tombs of Mevlevi leaders, and some inscribed Ottoman tombstones.

Explore Arabahmet.

For a completely different sense of Nicosia, walk west into the quarter known in Turkish as **Arabahmet**. Many houses have huge covered balconies overhanging the street, decorated with Venetian shutters and supported by elaborate balustrades; most are in dire need of restoration.

In the east of this quarter is the huge, tastefully restored **Dervish Pasha mansion** (+90 392 227 3569) – once owned by the editor of the first Turkish-language newspaper in Cyprus, a copy of which is displayed. The mansion is typically 19th-century Cypriot, in that it's an L-shaped building arranged around a central courtyard – the courtyard is flanked by a light, airy colonnade, and there are exhibitions of Turkish glassware and ceramics; but most interesting is the coolness and charm of the first-floor reception room or *selamlik* where guests would have been welcomed. Remarkably, as you climb the staircase from the ground floor to the first floor, the construction material changes from stone to mud brick – it's barely perceptible, but it must have saved a penny or two when it was built.

Find an Armenian inscription.

The far west of Arabahmet is the **Armenian quarter** of the city – or at least it was until 1963/64, when the community was forced from the area by Turkish Cypriot fighters. Many of the houses here are now wrecks – and the once-enviable view across from the western walls to the Ledra Palace hotel now stretches across the UN buffer zone where there is a prominent watchtower; the hotel is now headquarters of the UN peacekeeping force.

Upon a wall near here, on Dervish Pasha street near the corner with Tanzimat – directly opposite the Women's Library and easy to miss – is a fascinating, Turkish-language **inscription** in Armenian script. There are three dates, 1791, 1801 and 1805, above what looks like a clockface. The reason for the dates is a mystery, but Alexander-Michael Hadjilyra has researched the building and discovered that it was occupied by an Armenian family probably as far back as the 19th century (see www.gibrahayer.com/index.php5?&page_id=157 and scroll down the page). The plaque is potential evidence of an Armenian presence in Nicosia perhaps a century earlier than that.

Coast to hills: Kyrenia and the Pentadaktylos

The long spine of the Pentadaktylos or "five finger mountain" – so named after Dighenis, the Byzantine epic hero, who in the legend, placed his hand on the mountain, leaving the indentation in the landscape – divides the baking hot plain of Mesaoria from the fertile, northern slopes of the Kyrenia region. The old, atmospheric harbour of Kyrenia, with its castle, is just the other side of the mountains from Nicosia – and is surrounded by monuments, from St Hilarion and Buffavento castles on the ridge, to the famous old Gothic abbey of Bellapais. Further east, Kantara Castle is the most isolated and romantic of the lot – partly thanks to the effort it takes to get there.

Have a drink on a boat in Kyrenia harbour.

There's no shortage of places to have a coffee or a beer in Kyrenia harbour – and no shortage of staff to try to lure you in – but if you're prepared to walk far enough, then perhaps the nicest coffee stop is the **Boat Cafe** at the far eastern end of the harbour, below the castle. This is a moored boat that doubles up as a cafe-bar, and here you can have a beer or a coffee as you bob on the waves, with views of the harbour to the west.

Visit the shipwreck museum in the castle.

Kyrenia Castle is a proper Venetian castle, with a huge square courtyard dotted with palms, and plenty of opportunity to wander on the battlements – but the real highlight of a trip here is the Shipwreck Museum housed within its grounds. Here are the remains of a ship that sank not far from Kyrenia, around 300 BC, found with around 400 amphorae of wine from Rhodes, along with almonds, figs, olives and grapes (identifiable by their seeds); 29 millstones were also used as ballast.

Kyrenia II, a reconstruction of the ship built as a work of experimental archaeology, can be seen at the Thalassa Museum of the Sea in Ayia Napa (page 77).

Visit Bellapais.

Of all the sights in the north, **Bellapais Abbey** (www.islebright.com/links/250cy/138) is probably the most famous – and, thanks to Lawrence Durrell's *Bitter Lemons of Cyprus*, the most evocative of a Cyprus only recently gone. The half-ruined arches of the old abbey stand slightly forlorn in an idyllic spot in the Pentadaktylos foothills, not far from the house where Durrell lived, with views down over Kyrenia itself. After visiting the old abbey, you could eat at the balcony bar-restaurant at Kybele, just outside the grounds.

Near the abbey is the Tree of Idleness, famously mentioned by Durrell – the legend being that anyone who drinks coffee under its branches is forever consumed by idleness.

Make the climb up to St Hilarion.

Just off the main Nicosia-Kyrenia highway, ruined **St Hilarion** (www.islebright.com/links/250cy/139) is the easiest of the Pentadaktylos castles to visit – if you discount the climb to the top, that is. Its multi-level battlements, built on ever more precipitous crags, give it a fairytale air – in the local folklore, it has been the inspiration for stories about the Rigaina or semi-mythical "Queen" of Cyprus who is said to have made her home here. Among the "royal apartments" at the top, the most striking room contains the so-called

Queen's Window – a Gothic arch overlooking a precipitous drop.

The most common story about St Hilarion is that this was a palace of 101 rooms, the 101st being the room where the Queen kept her treasure; a shepherd, so the story goes, once stumbled into the room – and woke up some years later amid the castle ruins.

Try to visit St Hilarion on the way to Kyrenia rather than on the way back, because the latter involves a nightmarish short-notice right turn off a fast dual carriageway.

If you have any energy left, climb Buffavento.

Higher even than St Hilarion, **Buffavento Castle** (www.islebright.com/links/250cy/140) offers fairytale views of the Pentadaktylos range as it sweeps away east towards Karpas – the many peaks appear to repeat themselves infinitely, as if you're viewing them from within a hall of mirrors. Again, it takes a while to get there: after passing through an intimidating gateway at a lower level, you just seem to keep climbing up and up the stone stairs, briefly stopping to peek into half-ruined rooms where goatherds have (judging by the evidence on the floor) sheltered their flocks. Many of the "Rigaina" stories associated with St Hilarion (see above) are also associated with Buffavento – which isn't surprising, as the ruins are strikingly similar.

Explore the Pentadaktylos trails.

Whether you are walking, mountain biking or have a 4x4 vehicle, the network of footpaths and rough **trails in the Kyrenia area** of the Pentadaktylos – particularly the areas south of Bellapais and west of St Hilarion Castle – merit exploration. A non-profit group, the Kyrenia Mountain Trail Association, has marked trails in the area (and not only here, but from Kormakitis in the west to Karpas in the east).

Find the old monastery of Ayios Ioannis Chrysostomos.

The empty shell of the monastery of **Ayios Ioannis Chrysostomos**, on the forested slopes of the Kyrenia mountains near Buffavento, is a lonely sight. The monastery was founded, according to some versions of local legend, by a Byzantine princess; and it must have once been picture-perfect, with its domes commanding views of the Mesaoria plain. The exterior of the monastery retains its beauty – but with the exception of some disturbing graffiti, the interior is now bare.

Protect the turtles at Alagadi beach.

It's a short but scenic drive down from the main Kyrenia-Karpas road to **Alagadi beach**, a major turtle nesting site, home to the main turtle conservation efforts in the north. It's possible to volunteer to assist the Marine Turtle Research Group (www.seaturtle.org/mtrg) here – work which involves monitoring females and nests. For casual visitors, the beach is a decent enough spot, but a bit marred by views of the Alagadi power station to the west.

See Kantara Castle.

Perhaps because of its position at the far east of the Pentadaktylos range, not as many people visit **Kantara**

Castle as its fame would seem to warrant. But it demands a visit, not only for the climb up at the top, its imposing medieval walls and its views east to the Karpas peninsula, but also for the general feel of the mountains in these parts. At Kantara village, to the west of here, there is a romantic "hill station" feel – to get the full flavour of it, I would recommend driving from south to north on a hot day, to get increasing relief from the heat as the road twists and turns through the pine trees.

From coast to hills: Karpas peninsula

Nowhere in Cyprus competes with Karpas for wild beauty – and that is saying something. The "panhandle" of Cyprus (as it is known, thanks to its appearance on the map) is a remote, isolated region – so isolated, in fact, that a small population of Greek Cypriots was able to remain here after 1974. Visitors will discover seemingly endless roads, beaches, coves, ridges, olive groves – and even, at the tip of Karpas, an enclosure for the wild donkeys that roam here.

Visit the monastery of Apostolos Andreas.

Whether or not your visit to **Apostolos Andreas** is strictly a pilgrimage, it will feel like one. You follow mile upon mile of roads – sometimes bumpy and potholed, sometimes modern; sometimes twisting and turning, sometimes straight as an arrow – and often, just when you think you must have arrived, another Karpasian vista of wild ridges, escarpments and hillocks stretches out in front of you. Occasionally, you'll find a taverna with a Greek name on it – evidence of some of the Greek Cypriots who remained in Karpas after the 1974 invasion, and despite the subsequent expulsion of many of the Greek Cypriots who remained.

When you finally arrive at the monastery itself, you'll find it dilapidated and probably surrounded by market stalls – but that doesn't in itself detract from the significance or isolated feel of the place. Arrive on a Sunday evening and you will, most likely, find a priest singing evensong alone.

Look out over the Golden Beach.

Karpas is famous for its beaches – and the most famous of all is the long, white beach known as **Golden Beach**. Perhaps the best viewpoint is from the entrance to the Karpas donkey enclosure, looking down at its full length and the coast sweeping round toward Famagusta; at ground level the beach isn't quite as idyllic, with the windswept dunes difficult to walk on, and the coast scattered with flotsam.

Visit the church of Ayios Philon.

The ruined church of **Ayios Philon**, on the north coast not far from Rizokarpaso (Turkish: Dipkarpaz), has one of the most romantic locations anywhere in Cyprus – and it is also steeped in history, being on the site of the ancient, largely unexcavated, Greco-Roman city of Karpasia. The church itself is a 10th-century ruin, though it occupies the site of a far older basilica with hexagonal floor tiles – there are deep holes on site, though, so be careful you don't put your foot in one. Next to the church is a rocky cove which is apparently the ancient harbour of Karpasia – and a little further down the coast via a dirt track, a sandy beach. To get here from Rizokarpaso, follow signs for the "Oasis at Ayfilon" hotel, right on the ancient harbour; or do as I did and just ask.

There are ruins of more early medieval churches further up the coast at **Aphendrika**, though I didn't make it this far myself; apparently Aphendrika was also an ancient city.

See the ruins of the Ayia Trias basilica.

Near the village of **Ayia Trias** (Turkish: Sipahi) – opposite an old house where white cows graze – are the thrilling ruins of a 5th or 6th century basilica. Wandering among these ruins as the sun sets to the west through the trees, you get a fantastic sense of being in an atmospheric, ancient shrine – though wild plants now grow in what was once the doorway, and the evening reverberates not to the sound of mass but to shepherds calling from nearby fields.

The remains of the walls still stand, though you can step over them, so it's possible to get a real sense of the floorplan – and excitingly, there are even floor mosaics here, with two pairs of sandals depicted alongside the Greek inscriptions and the geometric shapes.

Stop off at Panayia Kanakaria.

Just off the main road into Karpas, on the straight-as-a-die branch road towards Ayios Simeon and Galinoporni, the church of **Panayia Kanakaria** on the left of the road simply stops you in your tracks. This church, with its stone walls and terracotta domes, is best appreciated via an arched, stone gate on its western side; from here, the stone track that leads to the church leads the eye in.

The Panayia Kanakaria is most famous for its series of mosaic icons, which were looted after the 1974 invasion – many have since been recovered and returned to Cyprus, and can be seen in the Byzantine Art Museum, Nicosia (page 93).

See the caves of Ayios Simeon.

Not far east out of Ayios Simeon (Turkish: Avtepe) is a **large cave-tomb** high on the right, built into rocks very near the top of the ridge. According to the early 20th-century architect George Jeffery, the cave was well known in local folklore (apparently it was the military retreat of the Rigaina or semi-mythical "Queen") – and it attracted the attention of 19th-century explorers and antiquarians such as Sir Samuel Baker and David Hogarth. Jeffery describes the path to the cave as "exceedingly difficult", and I would concur, because it took me two visits even to locate the cave, only to run out of time before I could even try to get there.[8]

I did, however, get some last-minute advice from a friendly local. So if you want to visit before I do, head out of Ayios Simeon until, in open country, you find a road on the right marked "Keklik Sokak" on a wooden sign. If you follow this a short way, you will see a wooden waymarker on your left, which marks the start of the trail – but the path east across the field may be overgrown, in which case you should back up, head further along the road a short way, take the next track right and meet the path on the other side. The goal – probably easier said than done – is to continue broadly parallel to the paved road for a mile or so, gaining height all the while until you reach the caves. Take great care – and best of all, take advice locally before you go.

Famagusta and Salamis

Until 1974, Famagusta was a booming city – with a busy port, traditional historic centre and rapidly expanding coastal suburbs, not least the hotel strip at Varosha, south of the old walled city. After the 1974 Turkish invasion, however, Varosha was sealed off – and its mainly Greek Cypriot inhabitants were not allowed to return. These days the old city – which, for its part, had a mainly Turkish Cypriot population – has a quiet and at times eerie feel.

Not far from Famagusta is Salamis, one of the major archaeological sites of Cyprus, which should be on any all-island itinerary – and the old monastery of St Barnabas.

Visit the Gothic centre of Famagusta.

The historic centre of Famagusta remains romantic and photogenic, thanks to its architectural mixture of minarets, Gothic arches, flying buttresses and palm trees – but it's somewhat eerie, because its streets are quiet and most of its pre-Ottoman monuments are ruined or semi-ruined.

The city's main monument, the **Lala Mustafa Pasha** mosque, is itself a damaged Gothic cathedral, built in the 15th century by the Lusignans – look up at its huge, late medieval facade, and you'll see its great windowless arches, pointing into thin air. This is the historic centre of the city; in front of the facade is a **fig tree** that's reputed to be 700 years old.

Behind you as you face the facade are the ruins of the **Venetian palace** where Marcantonio Bragadin, last Venetian governor of the island, ruled Cyprus until the 1571 Ottoman conquest, when he met an ignominious end.

Nearby are a number of ruins – one in every direction you'd care to walk in, in fact. A short walk south via a buttress-cum-archway is **St George of the Greeks**, a spooky shell pockmarked with cannon-fire, once used by the Orthodox community of the city and boasting a much smaller Byzantine ruin tacked onto the side; about the same distance north, along the port road, are the Gothic arches of **St George of the Latins**; while west from the Venetian palace is the heavily buttressed **Church of Saints Peter and Paul**, later the Sinan Pasha mosque, which itself fell into disrepair.

Spot the Venetian lions at the Sea Gate...

The winged lion – symbol of Venice – is a recurring theme in Famagusta. The most famous of the lions (sadly wingless), near the **Sea Gate**, is a stone statue that is subject to a legend: apparently, once a year the lion opens its mouth, and anyone near it at the time can put their hand in and extract a treasure; the legend is perhaps associated with the riches that the Venetians were supposed to have left behind after the Ottomans invaded in 1571. A plaque of a winged lion is also on the seaward side of the gate, sadly inaccessible.

...and at Othello's Tower.

A winged lion can also be seen on a marble relief plaque above the entrance to the so-called **Othello's Tower**, a Venetian citadel romantically renamed by the British (in honour of the fact that Shakespeare's *Othello* was set in a Venetian "seaport in Cyprus", a historic setting that – given the fall of Famagusta in 1571 – accentuates the play's sense of gathering doom). As for the plaque, it's dated 1480 and honours "Nicolao Foscareno Cypri Praefecto", a Venetian governor responsible for the fortifications. Inside the citadel, it's possible to see the great medieval hall and climb up on the battlements.

Indulge your sweet tooth at Petek's.

Right near the seafront in the most historic part of Famagusta, **Petek's** patisserie (+90 392 366 7104, www.petekpastahanesi.com) is a bit of an institution. Among the tempting trays of sticky sweetness you'll find here, there's both *sutlu borek* (milk pie, known in Greek as *galakto-boureki*) and *loukoum sucuk* (Turkish delight sausage; don't worry, there's no meat in it). On the first floor, meanwhile, there is an unpretentious terrace which serves such delights as baked eggs with chilli – good for brunch – and stays open late as a cafe-bar. A sign on the outside quotes the poet Mevlana: "*Ne olursan ol yine gel*" ("Come, whoever you are, come").

Eat at Dezdemona's.

With an unbeatable location right in the city wall near the south-east corner of the old city, the **Dezdemona Kebab**

and Meze House looks like a great spot – despite the unfortunate name. The place serves kebabs until late, with a good, family atmosphere and traditional music.

See ancient Salamis.

The extensive ruins at **ancient Salamis** (www.famagusta.org.cy/default.asp?id=370) can be bewildering on a first visit, but are fascinating nevertheless. Most of what remains is Roman, from the huge theatre to the pillars of the gymnasium, not to mention some impressive baths and plumbing; but explore the site in full and you'll also see the remains of a Hellenistic agora and Byzantine basilicas too – including the large basilica of Ayios Epiphanios from around 400 AD. The far south-east of the site is isolated but evocative – here are the remains of an ancient harbour – and a beach runs the full length of the site, so it's even possible to swim.

Stop off at Ayios Barnabas.

Just west of ancient Salamis, the former monastery of **St Barnabas** is one of the most important pilgrimage sites for Greek Cypriots – it was the discovery of the body of St Barnabas here in 477 AD that caused the Church of Cyprus to be given autonomous status. Until the 1974 invasion, there were three elderly monks here, all brothers, and they stayed on briefly – but in 1976, they departed for the south. The church, whose interior is relatively intact, is now an icon and archaeology museum; it represents a relaxed and peaceful stop on the road from Salamis to the Pyla/Pergamos crossing.

Morphou and Kormakitis

Before 1974, Morphou was an almost entirely Greek Cypriot area. The region was always agricultural and was known as the "breadbasket" of Cyprus – but today it has a distinct back-of-beyond feel. It's worth visiting for the Greek Orthodox church of Ayios Mamas; and as a stopover on the way to Cape Kormakitis, an area known for its population of Maronite Cypriots, some of whom remained in their main village, Kormakitis, after 1974.

Visit the church of Ayios Mamas, Morphou.

In Morphou (Turkish: Guzelyurt), follow the signs for the "museum" and you will arrive at the 16th-century **church of Ayios Mamas** – known as the patron saint of tax avoiders, after a spat with Ottoman tax authorities that ended (to cut a short story even shorter) with him riding off on a lion. The church has an elaborate icon screen, made not only of wood but of marble, while the painted pillars depict Peter and Paul. The supposed tomb of Ayios Mamas is on the left as you go in.

The church is next to the local **museum** whose exhibits range from the sublime (the Golden Leaves of Soli, a recently excavated golden crown) to the ridiculous (a display of stuffed animals which includes a two-headed sheep).

Explore the Maronite village at Kormakitis.

The village of **Kormakitis** (Maronite: Kourmajit; Turkish: Korucam; www.maronitesofcyprus.com) is home to a sizeable community of Maronites – a Roman Catholic minority with a long history in Cyprus, who speak their own language (Cypriot Maronite Arabic) and sing in Aramaic in church. Most Maronites left the north in the wake of the 1974 invasion – but many remained, and in recent years others have returned to live. The village tends to fill up at weekends with visitors from the south.

In Kormakitis, try to get access to the **Maronite Cultural Centre** – a fantastic museum, visible on your left on the way in, but usually kept locked. As an English speaker, your best bet is to ask at the Village Wine House, a couple of streets back from the main road; they will know who has the key. It's worth the effort: as well as being one of the best organised rural museums on the island – with exhibits properly labelled, rather than thrown together and made to look pretty – it is also one of the most interesting, acting as a record of a minority population through the centuries. John Pahita, who manages the museum, is an engaging host.

Back at the **Village Wine House** (+90 533 881 8993), you can order a traditional lemonade and even buy a map of Cape Kormakitis, which marks all the tracks in the area, as well as caves and old tombs.

See St George's chapel on the coast.

The tiny little Maronite **chapel of St George**, dating from the 19th century, stands on a stretch of sand linking an offshore rock to the mainland – and is a beauty spot that rivals even Aphrodite's Rock. To get here, drive down to Cape Kormakitis until you reach Livera (Maronite: Pourj; Turkish: Sadrazamkoy), then take the road that hugs the coast, heading eastward again. Maronites come here every November to pray for winter rain; the rest of the time, you can stand, often alone, and marvel at the views out to sea and of the mountains of the Pentadaktylos rising steeply to the east.

The road from Kato Pyrgos: Vouni and Soli

The most recent Green Line crossing point to open is the Limnitis crossing, near Kato Pyrgos, which gives access across the Green Line from the Paphos/Polis area to two ancient sites on Morphou bay in the north – the castle at Vouni and the ancient city of Soli. At Vouni, in particular, you can visit outside high season and have the whole place to yourself.

Buy fruit from a roadside seller.

The road east from the Limnitis crossing is characterised by a sight you used to see a lot of in Cyprus, but don't much in the south any more – people **selling strawberries** by the side of the road, especially in spring when they're in season. Happily, the road isn't so wide and fast that you won't be tempted to stop.

Take the winding road up to Vouni.

Built 2,500 years ago as a military stronghold overlooking the ancient city of Soli, the **palace of Vouni** is a lonely hilltop site with views north over the Mediterranean Sea. To understand its history, you'd have to have a handle on the politics of the Cypriot kingdoms of the 5th century BC – suffice to say it was built by pro-Persian Marionites, then conquered by pro-Athenian Solians who subsequently became pro-Persian themselves – but its end was swift, as it was destroyed in 380 BC by fire. The most striking part of the site these days is a stone *stele* (slab) which stands at the end of an atmospheric courtyard – and the fact that if you drive up here, then (with the exception of the warden in his hut) you're very likely to be alone.

Check out the mosaics at Soli.

By comparison to the palace of Vouni, **ancient Soli** lacks a bit of atmosphere – but then anywhere would. The main site is encased under a workaday protective structure that's just begging to be revamped – but unlike Vouni, Soli lasted for 1,200 years, from its time as a Cypriot kingdom, via the Roman period, to early Christianity. The main sights here are a restored theatre, and some early Christian mosaics in a basilica, in geometric patterns and in the shape of a bird.

7. Things to do anywhere on the island

Of course, there's plenty to do in Cyprus that can't be done in any one specific spot. From land to sea, whether you're sport or arty, interested in wildlife or local culture, here's a roundup of things to enjoy – wherever in the island you happen to be.

Sport and leisure

Getting out into the countryside – on foot, on two wheels or on horseback – is one of the great pleasures of a holiday to Cyprus; hills, mountains and sea are all playgrounds for active types.

Go for a run (seriously).
Fancy running a marathon or half-marathon in Cyprus? The **Cyprus Marathon** (www.cyprusmarathon.com) takes place

each year in spring, while the **Aphrodite half-marathon and 5K race** (www.runclub.com.cy) is an autumn event. Both take place in the Paphos region of the island.

Go for a run (not as seriously).

Styling itself as a "drinking club with a running problem", the **Hash House Harriers** is a worldwide organisation with strong links to the British expat scene – and, therefore, an inevitable following in Cyprus. Devotees, ranging from fast runners to fit walkers, follow trails across the countryside laid by a "hare" – but the trails go missing in places and there are false trails aplenty, allowing the slowest of the group to catch up with the fastest. There is a general culture of giving silly nicknames and singing silly songs – but it's a way to get out and about in lesser-known places.

For a list of hashes in Cyprus (most, but not all, are family-friendly), browse the links at www.europe.harrier.ch /CY/CY.html.

Have a go at trail running.

Fancy a bit of wild running – on beaches, in pine forests and on mountain trails, all over the island? Then look up the **Cyprus Trail Runners**, who – judging by their Facebook page (www.facebook.com/pages/Cyprus-Trail-Runners/ 177277931611) – seem like an active and friendly bunch.

Go on a guided walk.

From autumn to spring, Cyprus is a fantastic country to walk in – but beyond the official nature trails, wayfinding can be tricky, and there's also hunting season to contend with, lasting from November to March. Solution? Walk with a guide. **Cyprus Walks Etc** (www.cypruswalksetc.com) offers a great range of scheduled and customised walks, with information also available for an independent, self-guided walk too.

If you prefer to walk unguided, check out **WalkCyprus.com** (www.walkcyprus.com), which offers maps and descriptions of a range of Cyprus trails.

Get on your bike.

Cyprus is heaven for road and mountain bikers alike – though unofficially speaking, most biking is mountain biking here. For road bikers, the **Tour of Cyprus** cycling challenge (www.tourofcyprus.com) is a three-day grand tour of the island taking you from Nicosia to Paphos – via Larnaca, Limassol and the Troodos mountains (twice). Mountain bikers, meanwhile, should look up **Mountain Bike Cyprus** (+357 26 432033, www.mountainbikecyprus.com), who offer tours to Troodos in summer or the Akamas peninsula in winter.

Go geocaching.

It's completely nerdy, but **geocaching** – the outdoor activity in which you find "caches" hidden at known GPS locations – is a good way to discover a hidden part of any country. You simply enter the details into your GPS device, then head out into the countryside (or town) looking for the cache. There are caches all over Cyprus, from Katopaphos to the Karpas peninsula – see www.geocaching.com for information.

Go for a ride.

There are plenty of ways to go **horse-riding** in Cyprus, but two stand out. The first is the Drapia Horse Farm near Kalavasos, up in the hills between Larnaca and Limassol, where you can ride through Cyprus' famous countryside and stay in traditional village accommodation too – see **Cyprus Villages** (www.cyprusvillages.com.cy) for more info. Or you could try **Ride in Cyprus** (www.rideincyprus.com) who offer overnight treks and casual rides, plus their "signature ride" which takes you along the "Venetian camel trail" to the Venetian bridges in the Paphos district; accommodation is arrangeable, too.

Cheer on the Moufflons.

The **Cyprus rugby union team** – known as the Moufflons – has only been around since 2007, but is flying high and making its way up through the international leagues. The team plays its matches at the Paphiako stadium, Paphos; see www.cyprus-rugby.com for info.

Go kitesurfing.

Many of Cyprus' southern beaches are wild and windswept – not ideal for swimmers, but a great place for kitesurfers to practise their skills. See **Kiteboarding Cyprus** (www.kiteboardingcyprus.com) for info on lessons – and the best beaches for beginners and the experienced alike.

Watch the Cyprus Rally.

Not surprisingly considering the endless, dusty gravel trails criss-crossing the interior of the island, Cyprus is a popular spot for rally driving – with the regular **Cyprus Rally** (www.cyprusrally.com.cy) even acting as a stage of the World Rally Championship from 2000-06 and again in 2009.

Just get out and explore the map.

There's no limit to what you can do in Cyprus if you're armed with a decent map – getting out and visiting little villages with strange, polysyllabic names in the middle of nowhere is half the fun of going abroad. But for this purpose, you can't really rely on the maps doled out by the CTO (Cyprus Tourist Office), helpful as they are for the overview they provide.

For enjoyable exploration, I would recommend the *Reise Know How Map: Zypern* (*Zypern* is German for Cyprus); although dated 2010, it's more up to date than some maps published later.

Alternatively, the *Insight Flexi Map* is surprisingly clear and detailed for its small scale, showing the exact location of even isolated sights.

Wildlife

In Cyprus you can meet a huge range of unusual wildlife without really trying – from reptiles such as lizards, geckos and snakes, to insects such as *tsitsikes* (cicadas) which make such a racket in summer, to countless species of migratory birds. Here are a few ways to plan your holiday around Cypriot wildlife.

Go birding.
From flamingos in Larnaca's salt lake (page 70) to increasingly rare sightings of griffon vultures in Episkopi, Cyprus is a great spot for **birdwatching**. **BirdLife Cyprus** (www.birdlifecyprus.org) is a fantastic resource with info on where to watch birds in Cyprus – while companies such as Limosa (+44 1692 580623, www.limosaholidays.co.uk) and The Travelling Naturalist (+44 1305 267994, www.naturalist.co.uk/tours/cyprus.php) also organise tours.

Go on a turtle watch.
The isolated beaches of Cyprus are a breeding and nesting ground for both green and loggerhead **turtles** – but thanks to tourist development, many nesting grounds are lost and others are under threat. On the west coast, the Lara Turtle Conservation Project protects turtles at Lara beach, while nesting grounds in the Sovereign Base Areas (British territory) are monitored by volunteers from Episkopi Turtle Watch (www.episkopiturtlewatch.com). In the north, meanwhile, there's an established project (www.seaturtle.org/mtrg) attracting volunteers who are mainly students from Exeter University.

The arts

From traditional crafts to modern artists, there is a surprisingly active art scene in Cyprus – while for literary types, there is also a good deal of classic travel writing to get your teeth into, too.

Indulge your crafty side.

One thing visitors always love about traditional, Cyprus restaurants are the woven chairs you sit on – which look fantastic even in a modern home. There is a **chair-making workshop** in the western Troodos village of Phoini (www.phinivillage.com).

Make a Cyprus mosaic.

Thanks to the Roman examples at Paphos and Curium, Cyprus is famous for its mosaics – and it's possible to learn **mosaic-making** in plenty of places on the island. Examples include A Touch of Glass (www.maliaglass.com), a glass and mosaic workshop in the village of Malia, Limassol district; or the Mosaic Collective (www.mosaic-collective.net) in central Limassol.

Discover Cyprus artists

I've already mentioned Open Studios Nicosia (page 92), a bicommunal art exhibition which throws open the doors of artists' studios in the capital. But elsewhere in the island, there's also the **Open Studios Cyprus** (www.openstudioscy.com) project, which covers just the Paphos, Polis and Limassol districts. The scheme runs during weekends in October – and the good news is that many of the artists are based in villages, so, armed with a downloadable map of the exhibition, it's a great excuse to tour from one village to another with at least some vague purpose in mind.

See also the entries on pottery in Lemba (page 17) and Larnaca (page 73); the opera at the Paphos Aphrodite

Festival (page 16); and on Hambis Printmaking Museum (page 45) in the village of Platanisteia (also known as Plataniskeia).

Pack (or download) some holiday reading.

For many people, good holiday reading is a decent crime thriller or trashy novel for the beach. If you want to find out more about the island, however, here are a few books to bring with you (or download to your ebook reader):

- For background on the troubles of the 1950s, Lawrence Durrell's *Bitter Lemons of Cyprus* is essential reading – it's funny and heartbreaking in equal measure.
- For a romantic, meandering portrait of what Cyprus was like before 1974, Colin Thubron's *Journey into Cyprus* is a bittersweet joy.
- For a view of Cyprus past, try to pick up an old copy of *Romantic Cyprus*, by Kevork K Keshishian – which ran into countless editions but ceased publication in the early 1990s. You could buy a copy on eBay or try to track it down in the Moufflon bookshop, Nicosia.
- For a personal tour of the post-classical ruins of the island, Gwynneth der Parthog's *Byzantine and Medieval Cyprus: A Guide to the Monuments* is a great book if you can find a copy.
- If you can find it, *Cyprus 1878: The Journal of Sir Garnet Wolsey* is a gloriously un-PC private portrait of British colonialism by the first governor of Cyprus.
- *Cyprus As I Saw It in 1879* by the explorer Samuel Baker, available as an ebook, gives an insight into 19th-century Cyprus.

- For a portrait of how division, extremism and mistrust have tainted the island, *Echoes from the Dead Zone* by anthropologist Yiannis Papadakis is a must-read.

Cyprus culture

From Middle Eastern card games to Byzantine rites to hangovers from British colonialism, Cypriot culture draws from a hotch-potch of global influences.

Ride on a Bedford bus.

Formerly one of the great motoring symbols of Cyprus, traditional **Bedford buses** would once ply the routes daily between the towns and the mountain villages – with passengers inside and their luggage thrown on top of the roof. These days, there are only a few of the buses left in service, mainly providing transport for wedding guests – so if you're lucky enough to get invited to a wedding in Cyprus, you might get the chance to climb aboard one.

Discover British throwbacks.

There are reminders of **British rule** all over Cyprus – from British-style postboxes (now painted yellow, not red) to the chips on the side of your plate. But one of the most interesting traces are concrete water fountains – often marked with a simple royal inscription and year, such as "ER 1953" – which can be found in may out-of-the-way villages. I have often thought it would be an interesting, and ever so slightly geeky, project to catalogue them all.

Celebrate a religious festival.

For Greek Cypriots, **religious festivals** are a very big deal indeed – and there are some at practically every time of year. You could head down to the beach at Epiphany (January 6) to see priests throwing a cross into the waves; join in the traditional kite-flying on **Kathara Deftera** (Clean Monday; usually in March or April), a day when many villages, particularly Yeroskipou near Paphos, organise events to celebrate; or even have Christmas in Cyprus.

But the biggest deal of all is Greek Easter Sunday – and particularly midnight mass on Saturday night. Each year at this time, the Greek Cypriot youth is gripped by a collective pyromania, building huge bonfires near churches and amusing themselves by throwing fireworks and other explosives into the flames – but this perilous sideshow aside, it's worth trying to get to a village church, where, at midnight, the "holy flame" is brought out by the priest and spreads out through the candles of the congregation. Then, on Sunday morning, Greek Cypriots break their Lent fast with *flaouna*, a type of cheesy bread made with mint and spices, and dyed hard-boiled eggs.

Remember that Greek Easter isn't always the same date as western Easter, so check your dates!

Take a service taxi.

In days gone by, cars were beyond the reach of many Cypriots, so there was only one way to get from town to town in Cyprus: by **service taxi**. You called the taxi company, and within half an hour a big Mercedes with a three-litre engine, automatic driveline and three banks of leather seating would turn up at your address – upon which you piled in, and proceeded to sweat profusely into the back seat as the driver (who listened to only traditional Cyprus music, turned up very loud) proceeded to go round all the other houses of all his other pickups in the town, finally proceeding on his journey when the taxi was full. At the next town, the whole rigmarole would be completed in reverse, until you were let out (inevitably last); and if you wanted to cross the island from, say, Paphos to Larnaca, then you did the whole thing twice, changing in Limassol half-way. Yes, it could take all day – but it was sociable, economical, effective and not a little fun.

These days there is a motorway with inter-city buses on it (www.intercity-buses.com), and everybody has a car – but there is still a service taxi company plying its trade. It's called Travel & Express (+357 7777 7474, www.travelexpress.com.cy) – and it runs its service in blue Mercedes vans, which double up as courier vehicles. The system is still broadly the same, and if you choose this way of getting around, you'll see a side of the country most people don't glimpse.

In the coffee shop, try to keep up with the tavli...

In coffee shops in Cyprus, you'll often find locals playing **tavli** – a form of backgammon. Try to get a regular to teach you; as backgammon website Bkgm.com explains (www.bkgm.com/variants/Tavli.html), there are apparently three variants, *portes*, *plakoto* and *fevga*, each of which is played in turn, and usually at high speed.

...or teach yourself spastra.

There is also a coffee shop card game called **spastra**, widely known in Cyprus and perhaps the best card game I know for two players. A "fishing" game, it rewards players who can take all the cards left on the table, using mathematical combinations. For the rules, see the Wikipedia page about *bastra* (http://en.wikipedia.org/wiki/Bastra), another name for the same game. It's quite diverting on those holiday nights when there's just two of you, a pack of cards and a bottle of wine.

Which leads us neatly on to...

Food and drink

From coffee shop to taverna to bakery on the corner, eating and drinking are essential elements of Cyprus culture.

At the coffee shop

In every village in Cyprus, you'll still see groups of people – usually older men – sitting outside the *kafeneio* or coffee shop. You'll probably get a friendly welcome if you stop to join them; just don't expect to pay for your own coffee.

Drink traditional Cyprus coffee ...

Cyprus coffee is an institution. It comes thick, short and black with a glass of water on the side, and the only choice is the amount of sugar you get with it: in Greek, *sketo* means no sugar, *metrio* means some sugar, while *glyko* means sweet. Be careful not to drain the cup when you drink, as the bottom of the cup still contains the coffee grounds.

... or cool down with a frappe.

An alternative on a hot day is **frappe** – a foaming, iced drink made from instant coffee, and just the thing to order in a beach bar. If you become addicted to *frappe* – easily done – you can go to a DIY store and buy a "frappediser", which foams up your coffee with minimal effort.

Have your fortune told from coffee grounds.

Here's a tradition to enjoy if you have a spare five minutes in a coffee shop. When you've finished drinking your coffee, put the saucer on top of it, then invert cup and saucer together and wait for a few minutes. Then, invite a friend to take the coffee cup and **read your fortune** in the grounds.

There are a few traditions associated with this. First, if your cup sticks to the saucer when you remove it, somebody loves you; if there are a lot of speckles, you are going to be rich; "paths" in the coffee grounds, leading up from the bottom of the cup, are supposed to be possible paths in which your life might take; and, of course, it is considered bad luck to see your own cup: somebody else must do it for you.

Hint: don't try this with a *frappe*, or you will get ice all over the table.

At the table

Eating is the thing you will probably spend most time doing in Cyprus – and that often means having a full-blown *meze*.

The principle of a *meze* is the sharing, the feasting, and eating lots of little "starters" rather than having all your food dumped in front of you in one go.

Have a crack at the olives.

If you're a foodie, you'll probably already know that some of the best Greek olives are the rich, plump, black *kalamata* olives. You can certainly find these in Cypriot supermarkets, but traditional **Cypriot olives** are completely different: they're green olives, picked young and served cracked (Greek: *tsakistes*) with coriander seeds, lemon and garlic.

Fill up on flowers.

Courgette flowers (Greek: *anthoi*), whether deep-fried or stuffed with Cypriot cheese and a hint of mint, are a springtime treat. You may see the delicate and bright yellow flowers piled in boxes in supermarkets – or they sometimes appear as part of the meze in good restaurants, such as Stou Kyr Yianni (page 47) in Omodos.

Dive into the dips – especially when they're home-made.

Dips such as *tahini* (Turkish: *tahin*; sesame seeds) and *tsatsiki* (Turkish: *cacik*; yogurt with garlic and cucumber) are a Cypriot mainstay. Sadly, not many restaurants seem to make them themselves – but when they do, they're likely to be made from better quality oil and taste better. Note that even if you don't order a dip, the more hospitable restaurants may well bring one to your table in any case, along with a few olives.

Let halloumi melt in your mouth.

I've never met anyone who doesn't like grilled **halloumi** – known in Turkish as *hellim*. This pan-Cypriot cheese is rubbery when uncooked – but a few minutes on the grill turn it into a melt-in-the-mouth joy. It is also enjoyed cold for breakfast, when it goes surprisingly well with watermelon.

Learn to love loukaniko.

Like many countries, Cyprus has a proud tradition of **smoked meats** – which are often served as part of a *meze*, between the dips and the main course. *Loukaniko*, the best known of these, is Cyprus pork sausage, often richly spiced. There's also *pastourma* (Turkish: *pastirma*), which is smoked beef, and even *tsamarella*, smoked goat rump, which is excellent with a cold beer after you've been out for the day. Finally, it's not possible to cover Cypriot smoked meats without mentioning *lountza*, a ham ubiquitous in the south – often served in a sandwich with *halloumi* or, in resorts, in lieu of bacon in an English breakfast!

Order anything with aubergines.

You can't usually go wrong ordering an aubergine-based dish in Cyprus. The Turkish classic **imam bayildi** – literally "the priest fainted" – is an aubergine stuffed with tomato, onion, aubergine pulp and plenty of olive oil.

In winter, slurp up the soup.

Cypriot soups may be little known, but in the mountains in particular, **trahanas** – made with soured milk, crushed wheat, lemon juice and yoghurt – can be a warming treat.

Follow the smoke signals.

On weekends, high days and holidays, taverna owners often wheel out the grill – by which I mean the barbecue – so this is the time to turn up if you want traditionally **grilled meats**. *Souvla* is the mainstay of Greek Cypriot cooking – serious chunks of lamb, grilled for a long time on a spit over a low heat. Turkish Cypriots, on the other hand, tend to cook kebab (smaller chunks of meat) – but either way, if the spit is turning, you're on to a good thing.

Try wine-soaked meats.

The tannin astringency of **krasato** – pork marinated in red wine – is an acquired taste, but a rewarding one. Its presence on the menu is a bonus, because it's a sign that the restaurant owner enjoys cooking traditional food. It seems especially popular in the Limassol wine villages.

When ordering fish, go local.

Picking Mediterranean varieties is a good starting point with **fish**. So avoid cod and plaice, which will have been frozen; instead order sea bass, sea bream (often farmed in Greece) or red mullet. Squid, octopus and cuttlefish are usually frozen, unless you're at a specialist fish restaurant, in which case they could be among the best things on the menu.

Cypriot booze

For most people, alcoholic drinks in Cyprus will usually mean a large bottle or two of Keo or Efes (Greek Cypriot and Turkish beers, respectively) served with a relaxed meal in company. But there are a few other typically Cypriot drinks to try.

At cocktail hour, have a brandy sour.

Sometimes known as the "national drink" of Cyprus, the **brandy sour** was supposedly developed during the 1930s in the Forest Park Hotel, Troodos, for the young King Farouk of Egypt. The drink is a cocktail of Cyprus brandy, bitters, lemonade and bittersweet lemon cordial – and is best served just as the shadows get long at five o'clock.

Discover xynisteri – and other native wines.

Cyprus is an ancient wine-making country with its own, **native grapes**. The best-known Cypriot grape is *xynisteri*, from which we get fresh, summery whites; good reds also come from *maratheftiko*, also known as *vamvakada*.[4]

Forget ouzo: knock back a zivaneia.

Every country has its firewater, and in Cyprus it's not ouzo but **zivaneia** (Turkish: *zivaniya*), a drink similar to *grappa*, made from distilled grape pomace. Some tavernas dole out *zivaneia* after a meal, but this practice is not nearly as common as in Crete, where the local equivalent, *raki*, is hardly ever paid for outside a shop (in Crete, I was once offered complimentary *raki* after buying an ice cream – and they wonder why Greece is in economic trouble. But I digress).

Try a Filfar.

Filfar is a brand of **orange liqueur** I hadn't even heard of until, one day, a restaurant owner in Pedoulas suggested I try it. Apparently, it comes from a recipe dreamed up by a Greek Cypriot working for the British Army in Famagusta in the 1940s. Try it and see what you think.

Fortify yourself with a commandaria.

Famous for centuries, sweet, red, fortified **commandaria** wine is – in my opinion – utterly underrated, and utterly delicious with ice cream.

Cyprus sweets

Cypriots love sweet things: try and track down each of the following delights.

Have a mouthful of galaktoboureki.

Well, I said it was a mouthful. And a finer, sweeter-tasting mouthful you couldn't possibly hope to find in Cyprus. **Galaktoboureki** (Turkish: *sutlu borek*) is a cold dairy pudding with layers of filo pastry on top.

Spoon out the spoon sweets.

Sticky **spoon sweets** (Greek: *glyka*) are a Cyprus speciality. Anything – nuts, cherries, oranges, lemons – is liable to be boiled in syrup to create the sweets, which are then served on a spoon with a Cyprus coffee on the side.

Try mahalepi – the blancmange of Cyprus.

Divine on a summer's day, **mahalepi** (Turkish: *mahallebi*) is the simplest of all possible desserts: a white blancmange flavoured with a hint of rosewater and pistachios on top. It can be found in the most unpretentious of cafes – from the Buyuk Han to the public cafe of the Paphos district court – but is none the less refreshing for that, and you should try it.

Take home some carob honey.

Carob syrup may be an acquired taste, but mix it with honey to make **carob honey** (Greek: *haroupomeli*), and it becomes strangely palatable. You can find it in speciality food shops.

Seek out soutzouko.

Often seen hanging in lines at mountain festivals or outside monasteries, **soutzouko** (Turkish: *sucuk*) is a nutty-sweet "sausage" made of almonds dipped in mixed grape must and flour (the dipping mixture is known as *palouzes*, and is a dessert in itself). It's chewy and not a little addictive.

One last mouthful?

Ekmek kataifi (Turkish: *ekmek kadayifi*) is a kind of "death by pastry": a syrupy pastry base with a custardy topping on top. Look out for it at a restaurant – it tastes divine.

And that's as good a note to end on as any.

Footnotes

1. For practical reasons – the *de facto* partition of the island being just one of them – the areas on which these chapters are based do not correspond to the official regions of the Republic of Cyprus. For example, there is officially no Troodos region, but it makes sense to have a Troodos chapter in the book.

2. Some web links are too long or unwieldy to appear in print. Where this is the case, a link via www.islebright.com (the publisher's website) is listed instead, which should redirect to the correct external link.

3. Transliteration of place names from Greek to English is a fiendish business. This book eschews the official, recently standardised English spellings of Greek Cypriot place names (eg "Pafos", "Anogyra", "Lempa"), preferring instead the broadly phonetic spellings by which places have been known by English speakers for many years ("Paphos", "Anoyira", "Lemba"). This approach has the advantage that it makes pronouncing place names accurately much easier – "Ayios Yeoryios", for example, is a better pronunciation guide than the officially correct "Agios

Georgios" – but it has the disadvantage that the spelling of place names on official Cypriot maps and signs may differ slightly from what you see in this book. Where the official spelling is a major departure from its phonetic equivalent, and in the case of major towns, both spellings are supplied.

4. For more on Cyprus wines and wineries, I recommend Yiannos Konstantinou's Cyprus Wine Pages (www. cypruswinepages.com) – he is an authority on the subject, and also sells books via his website.

5. The full name of the British Overseas Territory on the island is "the Sovereign Base Areas of Akrotiri and Dhekelia" – often abbreviated as "the SBAs". The Akrotiri (western) SBA is just west of Limassol, and the Dhekelia (eastern) SBA is just east of Larnaca. There are no signs to warn you when you set foot in the SBAs, and (except where the eastern SBA abuts the Green Line) no physical border as such; only near actual military installations will you find fences barring your way. It can be difficult at times to know when you're on British territory and when on Cypriot.

6. Jeffery G, *A Description of the Historic Monuments of Cyprus*, reprint, Zeno, London, 1983, p306.

7. Obsidian is a naturally occurring volcanic glass.

8. Jeffery, p260.

More from Islebright Books & eBooks

Islebright Books & eBooks is a small-scale, high-quality publisher with a focus on travel, language and how-to guides. More books about travel, Cyprus and the Greek language are planned for 2012.

To find out more about Islebright's latest books – and for additional online content – visit **www.islebright.com**.

Printed in Great Britain
by Amazon.co.uk, Ltd.,
Marston Gate.